To Donna West,
Preach the Word!

Bob Russell
I Cor. 15:58

Praise for *After 50 Years of Ministry*

I have known and respected Bob Russell for almost thirty years. When I learned that he was finishing up a book about critical lessons learned over the course of his incredible ministry, I could not wait to read it. When he kindly sent me an advanced copy, I devoured it. There are golden nuggets of wisdom on every page. Bob's honesty is laudable and his insights penetrated my soul. I hope every leader will buy and benefit from this book as much as I did.

BILL HYBELS
Founding and senior pastor, Willow Creek Community Church, South Barrington, IL

This book is a gold mine. Every church leader should read, devour, ponder, and heed it. Bob Russell exemplifies a powerful, well-balanced ministry. This book captures the best of Bob. We are beneficiaries.

MAX LUCADO
Pastor at Oak Hills Church and bestselling author

Bob Russell has modeled a gospel ministry that glorifies God and strengthens the church—and he has done so now for more than five decades. This book is full of wisdom, maturity, and biblical reflection on the pastoral task. My hope is that every minister of the gospel, young and old, would profit from the wisdom of Bob Russell in this book and would imitate his patient, enduring, and Christ-exalting pattern of ministry.

R. ALBERT MOHLER JR.
President of the Southern Baptist Theological Seminary, Louisville, KY

What makes this book powerful is Bob's willingness to write so vulnerably about what he would do differently and what he would do the same. His vulnerability helped break through my defensiveness and be more honest with myself about what I need to do differently. If I could only recommend one book on practical pastoral leadership, it would be this one. No matter what your struggles or successes you will be encouraged and challenged.

KYLE IDLEMAN
Teaching pastor, Southeast Christian Church, Louisville, KY, and bestselling author of *Not a Fan*

Bob Russell is a genius at communicating. This book has won a permanent place on my bookshelf—I know I will be rereading it again and again. Bob's examples are clear, profound, and stick like Velcro. If anyone in ministry wants to succeed, they need to know their Bible and read this book!

MATTHEW SLEETH, MD
Author of *24/6* and executive director of Blessed Earth

For seventeen years I sat in the office beside Bob Russell's and learned so much about ministry and leadership from him. Now, with the help of this book you have the opportunity to pull up a chair and sharpen your ministry skills. If you want a balanced and effective ministry, then devour this book and glean from the best. Bob is the real deal and candidly shares what to do and what not to do. What you'll learn across the desk from him can ignite your leadership and perhaps even save your ministry.

DAVE STONE
Senior pastor, Southeast Christian Church, Louisville, KY

A master of personal candor and storytelling, my friend Bob Russell compresses a lifetime of learning into a short book, which is a must-read for every servant of the Lord. I want my minister-son to read and heed it. If preaching is "truth through personality," the light and heat of this extraordinary pastor-leader will reinforce and rebuke both the overwhelmed and the overconfident in ministry. I wish I had Bob's wit and wisdom to guide me when I began to pastor forty-five years ago.

HAYS WICKER
Senior pastor, First Baptist Church, Naples, FL

If smart people learn from their mistakes, then wise people learn from the mistakes of others as well. Bob Russell has given a gift to us in this book. He could (and does) write with authority on how to do ministry the right way. But he has also given us the opportunity to avoid the temptations that sabotage joy and fruitfulness. If you read this book at age seventy, you'll nod. If you read it at age forty-five, you'll make mid-course corrections that accelerate your ministry. If you read it at age twenty-five, you will avoid a world of hurt and move toward your maximum capacity for ministry sooner and for more enduring impact.

JOHN CHANDLER
Leader, Spence Network

The honesty of Bob's stories, and the wisdom he offers from his experience at Southeast Christian for forty years, make this book a must-read for every pastor. I wish I had this book fifteen years ago, so I'll be buying several copies to give to each of my staff members. This is absolutely one of the most practical books on ministry and preaching I've ever read!

ROY ROBERTSON
Senior pastor, Legacy Christian Church, Senoia, GA

If it were not for Bob Russell, my ministry wouldn't be where it is today. No matter if you are a veteran minister or a rookie, you will deeply benefit from Bob's wisdom about ministry. If you want to know how to serve the church Jesus loves, you should read this book.

TIM HARLOW
Senior pastor, Parkview Christian Church in Orland Park, IL, author of *Life on Mission: God's People Finding God's Heart for the World*

A long and fruitful ministry cannot be sustained without integrity, the kind of integrity that comes from an authentic walk with God. And when I think of that kind of integrity, I think of Bob Russell. Every minister needs to read this book. It will inspire us to preach what we live so people will want to live what we preach.

RICK ATCHLEY
Senior Teaching Minister, The Hills Church, North Richland Hills, TX

I have observed Bob Russell's life and ministry for over twenty-five years. This book is a must-read if you want to avoid mistakes and be successful in ministry over the long haul. Bob's wisdom, honesty, and leadership insights are priceless.

DON WILSON
Senior pastor, Christ's Church of the Valley, Peoria, AZ

Experience is the best teacher, and Bob Russell has learned invaluable lessons in his five decades in pastoral ministry. He has chosen to bless both novice and seasoned pastors by sharing the wisdom gleaned from his fifty years of service.

KEVIN W. COSBY
Senior pastor, St. Stephen Church, president, Simmons College of Kentucky

Wish I had this in my hands fifty years ago! This wisdom is gold, mined from a pastor's life of exemplary preaching and pastoral leadership. Powerful, practical, perceptive . . . a must-read.

JIM HENRY
Senior pastor, Downtown Baptist Church Orlando

It takes a great man to look back over his life and write about his mistakes. Bob Russell does that in a very transparent way before he tells about the success of the great ministry at Southeast Christian Church in Louisville, KY.

BEN MEROLD
Retired minister, Harvester Christian Church, St. Charles, MO

Young pastors, here's a chance to get a bird's-eye view of your ministry that otherwise isn't available until decades from now. Time spent reading this book could multiply the effectiveness and heart of God's ministry through you.

BRENT VAN HOOK
Lead pastor, First Church of the Nazarene, Wichita, KS

Bob Russell is the consummate mentor to pastors: both young and old, rookie and veteran. These groups along with many others will be informed, energized, and challenged by this transparent view into one of the most effective ministries of the last half-century. Another home run!

HOWARD BRAMMER
Pastor Emeritus, Traders Point Christian Church, Indianapolis, IN

Bob Russell has been an inspiring and successful pastor, leader, and friend for decades. He has invested heavily in leaders by helping them think about the future, lead well, and finish well. With this book we have a powerful tool in our hands to get better at what we do by learning from one of the finest men I know.

MARTY GRUBBS
Senior pastor, Crossings Community Church, Oklahoma City, OK

Bob Russell has been a friend to many, including myself, while guiding the next generation of preachers. Now, it is no surprise that he would provide more than five decades of his knowledge and experience within the generous pages of this terrific book! *After 50 Years of Ministry* is a must-have, no matter what stage you are in your own ministry.

DUDLEY RUTHERFORD
Senior pastor, Shepherd Church, Los Angeles, CA, and author of *Walls*

More than twenty-five years ago as a young pastor, I sat down with Bob Russell and peppered him with questions about exactly how I should go about leading a church. In those two hours Bob gave me advice that has shaped and guided me as a pastor and ultimately as a seminary professor who trains pastors. The principles he shares work in a church of 50 or 15,000. I am delighted to see the wisdom of a man who so greatly impacted my life available to anyone.

HERSHAEL W. YORK
Victor & Louise Lester Professor of Preaching, Southern Baptist Theological Seminary, Louisville, KY

Bob Russell is a rare gift to pastors! This book, *After 50 Years of Ministry*, powerfully illustrates why. With moving transparency, Bob writes about his failures as much as his successes for the benefit of others. Bob's humility and wisdom oozes from every page as he allows the reader to sit at his feet and learn from one of the most faithful, humble, and significant pastors of this modern era.

BRIAN CROFT
Senior pastor, Auburndale Baptist Church, Louisville, KY, and founder, Practical Shepherding

I've always claimed Bob as the best leader I've ever had in my ministry life and credit him for setting the high mark of faithful, expository preaching and connecting ancient truths with modern-day life. I love and thank Bob for what he's done for me as a leader, teacher, and pastor. I honestly would not be where I am without his leadership, example, teaching, and encouragement.

JIM BURGEN
Lead pastor, Flatirons Community Church, Lafayette, CO

My friend Bob Russell has been a source of encouragement and leadership, and a godly example to me for over thirty years. I've been waiting for the wisdom he would share as he looks back over his extraordinary ministry. This book was worth the wait!

CAM HUXFORD
Compassion Christian Church, Savannah, GA

BOB RUSSELL

50 AFTER YEARS OF MINISTRY

7 THINGS I'D DO **DIFFERENTLY** & 7 THINGS I'D DO THE **SAME**

MOODY PUBLISHERS
CHICAGO

Edited by Elizabeth Cody Newenhuyse
Interior design: Ragont Design
Cover design: Thinkpen Design
Cover image of church copyright © aastock / Shutterstock (48472969). All rights reserved.
Cover image of window copyright © CHAINFOTO24 / Shutterstock (197675669). All rights reserved.
Author photo credit: Lisa Russell

Library of Congress Cataloging-in-Publication Data

Names: Russell, Bob, 1943- author.
Title: After 50 years of ministry : 7 things I'd do differently and 7 things I'd do the same / Bob Russell.
Other titles: After fifty years of ministry
Description: Chicago : Moody Publishers, 2016. | Includes bibliographical references.
Identifiers: LCCN 2016008637 (print) | LCCN 2016009358 (ebook) | ISBN 9780802413840 | ISBN 9780802493712 ()
Subjects: LCSH: Pastoral theology.
Classification: LCC BV4011.3 .R87 2016 (print) | LCC BV4011.3 (ebook) | DDC 253--dc23
LC record available at http://lccn.loc.gov/2016008637

We hope you enjoy this book from Moody Publishers. Our goal is to provide high-quality, thought-provoking books and products that connect truth to your real needs and challenges. For more information on other books and products written and produced from a biblical perspective, go to www.moodypublishers.com or write to:

Moody Publishers
820 N. La Salle Boulevard
Chicago, IL 60610

1 3 5 7 9 10 8 6 4 2

Printed in the United States of America

Dedicated to the late John Foster:
caring elder, exceptional board chairman,
most effective volunteer executive pastor ever,
and my loyal friend.
You are greatly missed, my brother!

CONTENTS

FOREWORD

How would you like to sit down for a long conversation with a veteran Christian leader whose life and legacy influences tens of thousands of Christians and churches?

You could ask him anything and get honest, transparent answers filled with a lifetime of pastoral experience and then walk away with a renewed heart and determination to serve Christ happily and effectively for the rest of your life. You are holding that opportunity in your hand. In a church world filled with trends, fads, and craziness, it is so good to hear solid, balanced advice that comes straight out of Scripture and a life well lived over many years of successful and fruitful ministry. *After 50 Years of Ministry* is gold!

My friend Bob Russell's life of integrity and faithfulness is inspiring and inviting. This shows up again and again in this book. Looking back actually takes you forward in the pursuit of ministry God's way.

Bob Russell is a thoughtful, kindhearted Christian, but do not mistake Bob's laid-back personality for passivity. A fire burns in this man's life, which has ignited believers with faith through many years of consistency in service. Bob's former pastorate, Southeast Christian Church in Louisville, Kentucky, continues to grow today because it is built upon Christ and the Bible and upon solid foundations laid by Bob, who shepherded this dynamic congregation for forty years. Bob is one of the best pastoral leaders I've known, and probing this man's heart and mind is pastoral training at its very best. I absolutely love talking church with Bob because you get wisdom, experience, humor, and practical advice without hype or exaggeration.

In this book, you are invited to learn and grow as a person and a minister and to strengthen your convictions, deepen your love, develop your gifts, and fulfill your calling. Bob brings humility and honesty to the discussion which covers nearly every pastoral subject—preaching, evangelism, church growth, pastoral care, criticism, stewardship, marriage and family, crisis management, stress, staffing, longevity and much more. I'm telling you this book is ministry guidance at its best!

We are told thousands of ministers are dropping out of ministry because of discouragement or disqualification. Unfortunately, I've seen my share of failed, broken former pastors and ministers who are just grinding it out instead of finding fulfillment in life's highest calling. Ministry should be an incredibly rewarding experience. With the right resources, spiritual gifts, and opportunities you can change the world right where you are, serving God's church, shepherding His people, sharing the Gospel, teaching God's Word, and investing in eternity. Pastoral leadership is critical to our generation and beyond. Your leadership matters. Living and leaving a legacy of faith is the richest experience in life, and passing the baton to future God-called ministers is vital to the spiritual health of the churches. Godly counsel is greatly needed in our generation.

So I am grateful to introduce you to a book you will treasure. Don't just read the book. Mark it, underline it, and use it to take you onward and upward in life's most rewarding calling—the work of Jesus Christ.

For me, ministry has always been a joy—never a job. I am thankful for pastoral mentors, like Bob Russell, who set the pace for all of us and inspire us to do better. So sit down with this book like you would a friend, and soak up a lifetime of godly wisdom. Be encouraged and challenged to fulfill your calling God's way and finish your race with joy.

Therefore, my beloved brothers, be steadfast, immovable, always abounding in the work of the Lord, knowing that in the Lord your labor is not in vain (1 Corinthians 15:58 ESV).

JACK GRAHAM, PASTOR
Prestonwood Baptist Church
Plano, Texas

INTRODUCTION

One of our fifth-grade Sunday school classes was asked to write an encouraging note to their preacher. I've kept Kenny Ward's note for over thirty years. On the outside of a folded 8½" by 11" piece of paper he had drawn a stick figure standing on a platform in front of a microphone. The top read, "To: Bob Russell." Inside he had scrawled, "You have to be brave to be able to stand in front of thousands of people. I'm glad you're a preacher at this church and I think you do a wonderful job. I am praying that one of these times you don't mess up—Sincerely, Kenny Ward."

I suspect Kenny had overheard his parents expressing their concerns about their preacher. They had probably witnessed far too many ministerial failures—especially in high-profile ministries. So Kenny was echoing their concerns. His family wanted and needed a leader who consistently walked the talk.

Although I managed to minister to the same church for forty years, the truth is I messed up quite a few times. I'm thankful I didn't have a major moral failure that forced me to resign in disgrace and embarrass Kenny Ward and his family. But still, I did make numerous mistakes that I wish I could go back and correct. Knowing what I know now, I realize my ministry could have been a lot more effective if I had a do-over.

Not long ago I was asked to speak to a group of megachurch preachers on the subject "If I Could Do Ministry Again." They requested that I look back on my forty-year ministry at Southeast Christian Church in Louisville, Kentucky, and reflect on things I would do differently and things I'd repeat, if I could start all over again. That talk became the genesis of this book.

MINISTRY IS MUCH HARDER THAN IT LOOKS

We have a tendency to view other people's jobs in their public "glamor moments," overlooking the tedious effort that goes on behind the scenes—work that is essential for success.

We see a doctor after he performs a dramatic surgery that saves someone's life. He accepts the effusive praise from the patient's family, gets into his luxury car, and drives to his spacious home and we think, "Wow, it would be great to be a doctor." But we don't see the extra years of medical school, the government regulations, the patients who don't survive, the late-night emergency phone calls, and the occasional lawsuits that a doctor endures.

We see a high school basketball coach being carried off the floor following a state tournament victory and think, "Man, it would be great to be a coach and impact young lives and experience that kind of excitement and adoration." But we don't see the hours of lackluster practices, the late-night watching of game films, the angry phone calls from disgruntled parents, the surly and lazy athletes who test the coach's patience, the gut-wrenching losses. We just see the glamor moment.

Some people see a preacher standing before his congregation on Sunday morning teaching the Bible and encouraging the people to live for Christ and think, "I should have been a preacher! What a rewarding life! And you work just one day a week!" They don't see all the tedious and time-consuming effort behind the scenes. They don't see the week-by-week cramming to come up with a sermon, the exasperating breakdowns in communication with staff members, the family vacations that are interrupted with yet another emergency, the board member who has a complaint, or the volunteers that don't show up.

Ministry is hard. It's rewarding. It's a divine calling. It's gratifying. But it's a very difficult task day in and day out. We've probably all seen the statistics on pastors who leave the ministry, the state of clergy marriages, ministers who battle depression, and more. Some studies paint a very dark picture; others are rosier. But regardless of the numbers, the point is that the ministry is a high, holy, and *hard* calling.

"I MADE THAT SAME MISTAKE"

My son Rusty is a preacher in Port Charlotte, Florida. He texted me last Monday a little discouraged. "I used the phrase 'immaculate conception' incorrectly in a sermon yesterday and I'm going to have to correct it next week. Nuts!"

He had not checked on the Catholic Church's definition of that term. Catholics use "immaculate conception" to communicate the belief that Mary was a perpetual virgin. Rusty had used it to simply describe the virgin birth as something pristine and perfect. When someone corrected him after the morning service he was embarrassed that he hadn't understood it correctly.

I texted him, "I made the same mistake with that phrase years ago." He immediately shot back, "Good! It really encourages me that you made the same mistake."

It's strange how we often get more encouragement from learning someone with experience has failed than we do from hearing their success stories. Somehow we don't feel so alone in our inadequacy and we conclude, "If they made mistakes and survived maybe I can too. If they can keep playing hurt, I can too."

I can understand why some drop out of ministry and don't return. But why do the rest of us keep doing it? Why do we stay? It's primarily because we've received a divine calling. God called some of us dramatically and others were beckoned by a gentle whisper or by a series of divinely orchestrated circumstances. We stay in ministry because it's an assignment from our heavenly Father, and we dare not lose heart.

Most of us are quick to admit that there's much about ministry we love. What a privilege to preach the unsearchable riches of Christ week after week. What an honor to deal with the major issues of life as we study God's Word and prepare lessons containing eternal truth. How rewarding it is to counsel with God's people and shepherd them through the valley of the shadow of death. Like the apostle Paul we say, "Woe is me if I don't preach the Gospel." Sure there are criticisms, but there are also a lot of encouragements. Sure there are daily pressures and occasional setbacks, but there are many accomplishments and meaningful victories that absolutely warm the soul.

If I had my entire life to live over, I'd choose to be a preacher again. It's been extremely rewarding and gratifying. If I was to be surveyed on my feelings about the ministry, I would be listed with those pastors who said they felt happy and content on a regular basis with who they are in Christ, in their church, and in their home. Though I initially resisted God's call to preach the Gospel, once I started, I never looked back. I have loved being a preacher! I can't say I've loved every minute of it, but my overall experience has been joyful and rewarding.

But I could do ministry a lot better if I were given a second chance. As I look back on forty years of ministry at Southeast Christian Church in Louisville, I wish I got a mulligan like amateurs do in golf—a do-over after a poor shot, not counted on the scorecard. This book lists seven things I'd do differently and seven things I'd do pretty much the same way. They are written in hopes they will be a source of encouragement to some who are tempted to grow weary and lose heart. I pray my observations will inspire others to conclude, "If he can do it, I can do it too."

PART 1

*What I Would
Do Differently*

I▶ I WOULD MINISTER MORE BY FAITH AND LESS BY FEAR

Don't fear your weaknesses—God supplies all the strength you need. Be afraid of those moments when you think you are independently strong.

—PAUL DAVID TRIPP

God did some amazing things during the time I was pastor of Southeast Christian Church, but I was often a reluctant leader. Although I usually concealed my anxieties fairly well and I eventually became less apprehensive, fear was a character flaw I battled throughout my entire ministry.

Moses is the Old Testament character I identify with the most. When God called him to confront Pharaoh and demand the release of the Hebrew slaves, Moses was reluctant to obey. He was fearful. He couldn't see himself performing that role. He protested, "I'm not a good speaker." "No one will ever believe me." "Please send someone else."

Some mistakenly interpret insecurity as humility, but the two are vastly different. Insecurity is self-centered, while humility is God-centered. At the burning bush, the Lord did not commend

Moses for his reluctance to lead. He chastised him for his lack of faith. Humility is not self-consciousness; humility is discovering what gifts God has given to you and using them wholeheartedly for His glory, not your own.

But God was going to do more through Moses than he imagined . . . or wanted. I experienced similar apprehension, and the Lord had to remind me repeatedly to walk by faith, not by fear.

AN INTIMIDATING CALL

In 1966 when I was first called to become the minister of a new church in Louisville, Kentucky, I felt extremely inadequate and ill prepared. I grew up in the country, milking cows. Southeast Christian Church was in the suburbs of a large, sophisticated city. I grew up attending a very small church (forty people); although this new church was fairly small (around 125 people), it clearly had the potential to grow large. I only had a BA degree from a Bible college. This church had a number of PhDs and well-educated people sitting in the audience every Sunday.

I was so nervous for my trial sermon I must have rehearsed it aloud at least fifteen times. In high school I hated public speaking or even reading in front of a class. I would sometimes hyperventilate, I couldn't catch my breath and my voice would quiver. For years I feared reliving that embarrassing experience when I preached. Comedian Steven Wright once asked, "What happens if you get scared half to death twice?" I was scared half to death multiple times and still survived.

With God's help I got through the trial sermon without faltering. When I received a unanimous call to come to Louisville, I immediately accepted it. J. Oswald Sanders wrote, "When God calls us, we cannot refuse from a sense of inadequacy. Nobody is worthy of such trust."[1]

I imagined staying for five or six years and helping the church grow to 300–400 people. Today when people visit our campus that has a million square feet of buildings, and they witness more than 20,000 people attending worship services every weekend, they often say to me, "You must have had an incredible vision for this church." I often jokingly respond, "Well, thanks, but we're actually a little behind what I had envisioned."

The truth is my vision was very limited. One of my favorite passages of Scripture is Ephesians 3:20–21: "Now to him who is able to do immeasurably more than all we ask or imagine, according to his power that is at work within us, to him be glory in the church and in Christ Jesus throughout all generations, for ever and ever! Amen."

Once I began the Louisville ministry in June 1966 there was no one more stunned at what started happening at Southeast Christian than I. As I sowed the seed of God's Word, it began producing a bountiful harvest. The east end of Louisville was a fertile field and it was soon producing thirty, sixty and a hundredfold. I underestimated the power of God's Word. I underestimated my giftedness to preach. I underestimated what God could do with even a reluctant leader.

Perhaps if I had dreamed bigger dreams He could have done more. But I do know that I often went kicking and screaming into projects that were so obviously God's will that I had no option. I often felt such tension on Friday and Saturday about the upcoming sermon that I wasn't fun to live with. If I had more faith, I wouldn't

have been as apprehensive or as tense as I was. I could have enjoyed
His blessing more.

A STRESSFUL ASSIGNMENT

Ten years into my ministry I was invited to speak to a morning
session of the North American Christian Convention, the annual
gathering of leaders from Independent Christian Churches. At that
time it was a significant honor to be asked to speak to the entire
convention—especially for a guy not yet thirty-five years old. That
was almost unheard of. However, the thought of speaking to a
crowd of 4,000 of my peers terrified me. This is going to sound like
an exaggeration to people who think speaking came easily for me,
but it isn't. I was just getting used to preaching to 500 people in
my own church and the idea of speaking to a convention audience
sparked tremendous tension.

I agreed to do it because it was an honor and I am supposed to
walk through open doors—right? Besides, I had learned a definition of courage while playing
football in high school as a
140-pound quarterback that
stayed with me all my life.
"Courage is not the absence
of fear. Courage is action in
spite of fear." I wanted to be
courageous but I have to admit anxiety has often plagued me and
inhibited me before taking action.

He assured me the Lord would be with me and once I started, all butterflies would be gone. I wasn't so sure.

The closer the NACC date came the more I prepared and
the more nervous I became. I remember going to lunch with my

college roommate, Ron Eversole, and sharing my fears with him. He assured me the Lord would be with me and once I started all butterflies would be gone. I wasn't so sure.

On July 4, 1976, my wife, Judy, and I flew from Louisville to Denver, the site of the convention. It was the 200th anniversary of America's Declaration of Independence. We left near sundown and there was not a cloud in the sky. As darkness began to settle in, we could look down and see spectacular fireworks bursting above one small town after another. The entire nation was celebrating the birth of our country beneath us. It was a glorious spectacle but I didn't enjoy it as much as I should have because of the pressure of that speech hanging like a heavy cloud over my head.

Fear of tomorrow robs today of its joy. Fear makes us irritable and inhibits our personalities. Fear stifles the Holy Spirit in our lives. Fear minimizes leadership effectiveness. Fear blinds us to the goodness of God. Corrie ten Boom said, "Worry does not empty tomorrow of its sorrows. It empties today of its strength."[2]

We arrived in Denver late Sunday evening. On Monday morning I walked to the convention center to get a feel for the location where I'd be speaking later that week. When I walked into the arena hundreds of chairs were being set up and technicians were testing out the sound system. As I ambled up toward the platform a sound technician kept repeating, "Testing, one, two, three" over the PA system. Then he called to me, "Excuse me, sir, could you lend me a hand? Would you mind standing behind the podium and speaking for a few seconds so I can go hear it in the back of the room?"

I leaped at the chance to stand behind the podium and talk for a minute or two until he was satisfied and thanked me for my assistance. I walked away with a renewed confidence that afternoon. As my wife and I made our way back to the hotel I said, "Judy, I'm not one who flippantly says, 'The Lord caused this to happen.' But you know how anxious I've been and how I've prayed that the Lord will calm my nerves. It's just too much of a coincidence for me to come down here to this arena and the sound technician asks me to stand behind the podium and speak. I think that the Lord is assuring me that He's with me and I'm going to be okay."

When we got back to the hotel a few minutes later, I ran into Southeast Christian's worship leader in the lobby. I explained where I'd been and told him I'd even done some trial speaking behind the podium where I was going to preach. He burst out laughing and said, "Oh, no! You were in the room where the teen session takes place—the arena where you're speaking is much larger than that!" Suddenly my anxieties resurfaced, but the laughter at my mistake probably did more to calm my nerves than anything.

When Thursday morning came, the Lord answered my prayers and I discovered that what Ron Eversole said was true: After the first minute or so my nerves settled down, I became absorbed in what I wanted to say, and the audience responded well to the message. Most importantly God had been true to His promise, "I will never leave you nor forsake you" (Hebrews 13:5 ESV). When it was over I felt a tremendous sense of relief and was gratified that I had taken action in spite of fear.

Usually the basis of fear is too much concern over what people think and not enough trust in God's promises. When God told Jeremiah he had appointed him as a prophet to the nations, Jeremiah protested, "'Alas, Sovereign Lord,' I said, 'I do not know how to speak; I am too young.' But the Lord said to me, 'Do not say, "I am too young." You must go to everyone I send you to and say whatever I command you. Do not be afraid of them, for I am with you and will rescue you,' declares the Lord" (Jeremiah 1:6–8).

I wish I had consistently listened more to those promises of Scripture and less to the fears the enemy frequently whispered in my ear. I could have been a lot more pleasant to live with at home, and I would have enjoyed the challenges and opportunities that came my way. I could have been a more effective leader if I would have been less fearful and more joyful.

AN INVITATION TO WALK INTO THE LION'S DEN

In 1983, our church raised a million dollars in a single offering. The plan was to use that money as seed money to erect a new sanctuary on the twenty acres we had just purchased for relocation, a half-mile down the street from our present building. The story of our million-dollar offering was picked up by the local newspaper and then became a front-page story in *USA Today*. My picture was on the front of *USA Today* under the headline, "Churches' One Million Dollar Sundays."

A few days later I received a phone call from the producer of the *Phil Donahue Show* inviting me to appear on his television program to talk about "Raising Big Bucks for Churches." Phil Donahue in the eighties could be compared to HBO's Bill Maher today. He was definitely not favorable to the gospel. His producer said, "I want you to know in advance, there will be people on the same panel who will disagree with what you are doing."

The last thing in the world I wanted to do was to go on Phil Donahue and be attacked by him and his cronies. I was petrified at the idea. What if I stumbled and stammered or hyperventilated and quivered? I would embarrass the people who had sacrificed of their hard-earned money to advance God's kingdom. But was God wanting me to share His Word on national television? If so, I knew I should do it. Courage is not absence of fear but action in spite of fear.

I sought counsel from our elders about the invitation and after considerable discussion they advised me not to accept the offer. It would be too hostile an environment. It would be "casting your pearls before swine." (I was glad someone found a Scripture verse to relieve my guilt and justify my fears!) So I turned down the invitation. I still wonder if that was a cowardly decision. Perhaps if I hadn't been so apprehensive the elders would have responded differently. I think the apostle Paul would have gone.

Over the years I did accept other invitations to be on talk shows that were adversarial and to participate in events that were challenging. But I dreaded each opportunity. I repeatedly read Jesus' admonition about not worrying about what I was going to say but trust the Holy Spirit to provide the right words—but

> *Worry says, "I don't think He will be there when I need Him."*

somehow my faith was too small. I was always anxious. I wish I hadn't been apprehensive, because God was always true to His promise to provide.

Worry is a sin because it calls God a liar. God promises He will supply all our needs (Philippians 4:19). Worry says, "I don't think God will fulfill that promise." God says He is with us always (Matthew 28:20). Worry says, "I don't think He will be there when I need Him." God promises when we're called to testify before authorities, "Do not worry about what to say or how to say it. At that time you will be given what to say for it will not be you speaking but the Spirit of your Father speaking through you" (Matthew 10:18–20). Worry says I might say something really stupid.

Oswald Chambers wrote, "It's not only wrong to worry, it is infidelity, because worry means that we do not think that God can look after the details of our lives."[3] Faith is trusting God to fulfill His promises. Worry is disbelief and an insult to God. I wish I would have trusted more because over and over again I discovered God's promises are true.

A FAINTHEARTED DECISION
CONCERNING THE SIZE OF A NEW SANCTUARY

When our first relocation project began, I intentionally wasn't on the building committee. I hate long meetings, am not gifted in aesthetics, and have no passion for details, so I don't belong on a building committee. I'd also seen too many ministers become distracted and lose their focus during a building project. The preacher becomes a lightning rod for disagreement and after the building is built, his ministry is soon over.

"Your faith is too small. You preach. We'll build."

So I wasn't on the building committee. But I did communicate two requests to Jack Coffee, the chairman. I said, "I'd like the sanctuary seating to be in a semicircle and I'd like for it to seat no more than 1,500 people." I explained, "We're running a little over a thousand in attendance now in a building that seats 450. With 1,500 seats in the new auditorium we can accommodate 3,000 in dual services. I don't think we'll ever get any larger than that. But if we have more than 1,500 seats we will rattle around in the huge space on Sunday nights and Wednesday nights."

Jack raised an eyebrow, frowned at me and scolded, "Your faith is too small. You preach. We'll build." A few months later the building committee approved a sanctuary design that seated 2,500 people and I was not pleased. However, by the time we occupied that building two years later we had to have dual services and we averaged over 4,000 the first year. I wish my faith had been greater and my fears had been smaller.

AN UNEXPECTED CONFIDENCE BOOSTER

One winter in the early nineties I awakened in the middle of the night and was unable to sleep. I got up, went downstairs, and decided to watch a video of a sermon Chuck Colson had preached at Southeast about a year before. We had three services at the time and Chuck had agreed to preach for two of them. Due to his health challenges, Chuck requested that I preach the middle service that Sunday.

After watching the video of Chuck Colson's excellent sermon, I started to turn off the tape when suddenly my face appeared on the screen. We had made a special effort to video that morning (which had not been our practice), since we had a special guest. I didn't realize our tech crew had also taped my sermon as well.

Since I was still wide awake, I decided to watch it. I hadn't watched myself on video very often and that message was over a year old, so I didn't remember much about it. Most preachers will agree that it's easier to be objective about a message when you're not as familiar with its content.

As I watched and listened at three in the morning, I realized, "This is pretty good! Wow! This is better than I imagined it was at the time." When it was finished, I gulped and thought, "That's not me! That's not me! That's an anointing of the Holy Spirit! God speaks through me! He's doing more than I imagined!"

I'm not a frequent crier, but I couldn't hold back the tears that night. I hurried into a nearby bathroom and sobbed. I kept asking, "God, what have You done to me?" That experience was a big confidence booster to me, because that night I realized that while there are many preachers more talented than I, I was not a one-talent man who had been planted in a fertile field. God had really anointed me to preach and had given me the opportunity to preach in a fertile field. That meant I had a heavy responsibility. But I need not be afraid.

I wish I could say I've never had a moment of fear since, but I am a continual sinner. However, my faith has grown and my confidence is still growing even today. But I do wish I had less fear and more faith because "God is able to do immeasurably more than we ask or imagine."

A MASSIVE BUILDING PROGRAM
AND THE DREADED FUNDRAISER

In the early nineties Southeast Christian exploded to 6,000 people in worship on Sunday morning. We had already outgrown our new facilities in four years. We added a Saturday night service. We included a closed-circuit service in the fellowship hall. We were once again shuttling people who had to park at local schools and shopping centers.

Just four years after relocating, those of us in leadership began asking, "Could it be God's will for us to relocate again?" That was almost an unthinkable challenge at the time. We were still $3 million in debt. We had just barely had time to catch our breath and settle into our new building. The carpet still smelled new.

We began to pray and discuss the possibility of picking up our tents and moving on again. We put out several "fleeces" that we all agreed on. If we were to relocate we would need a hundred acres of ground adjacent to an intersection on the interstate. The price of the land would have to be less than $40,000 an acre. It would need to be within ten miles of our present site. We'd have to get overwhelming congregational approval. We would need to increase mission giving 1 percent per year during the construction project, beginning with the current practice of sharing 10 percent annually. That would demonstrate that we hadn't lost our outward focus.

We debated for a year about what was the right thing to do. On a staff retreat an associate minister said, "Bob, people are just waiting for you to take the lead and say, 'Let's go for it.' They're ready to follow you."

That night while praying in my room at the lodge I came to grips with the fact that was true. And that's a heavy burden. This was a HUGE step. Shortly afterward I sought the counsel of several ministers I deeply respected. Maybe I was still looking for a way out. But they each encouraged me to go for it. "We need someone paving the way," one of them said.

A relocation committee was formed. After a few months they announced that a hundred acres of land had become available at the intersection of I-64 and Blankenbaker Parkway, on the east side of Louisville. The cost of the land fell within our parameters. I remember my knees quaking as I announced to the church that we were going to vote in two weeks to purchase a hundred acres of ground for the purpose of relocating again. You could hear a pin drop.

Two weeks later the congregation voted 94 percent in favor of relocating. Many churches couldn't get 94 percent to vote in favor of Jesus returning! The land was purchased and an architect hired. Then came the step that makes almost every preacher apprehensive—a capital campaign.

Every preacher who has been through a building project wrestles with the fears. Are we walking by faith or being presumptuous? Will we retain the same spirit in the larger facility? Will I have to talk so much about money that the congregation will be turned off? Can we keep our focus on Christ and not the building?

We needed to raise $26 million over a three-year period for the financial package to work. We were told by our financial advisors that it was the largest church fundraiser they knew of at that time. Our annual budget then was $8 million dollars, so we were attempting to more than double our budget the next three years.

I got some discouraging notes in the mail from some knowledgeable businessmen. "I've done the numbers and they don't add up." "If we raise $26 million it will be the biggest miracle I've ever seen."

Our financial consultant insisted for the project to be successful I needed to do three things as the leader—none of which I wanted to do. (1) Preach four straight sermons on giving. (Wouldn't that be overkill?) (2) Approach twelve donors who had the potential to give leadership gifts and ask them for an advance, generous donation. (We could offend some of our most loyal givers.) (3) Announce to the congregation what I personally was going to pledge toward the project. (Wasn't that being boastful? Wasn't giving supposed to be in secret?)

But I agreed to follow the guidelines of the experts, and the capital campaign proved to be a tremendous blessing. Our congregation rallied and committed $31 million—$5 million over the goal, and amazingly, over 100 percent was donated. It ignited a spirit of revival in the church. Again, all my fears were unfounded.

In his older years Moses taught Joshua and the Israelites a lesson he had learned, "Be strong and courageous. Do not be afraid or terrified because of them, for the Lord your God goes with you; he will never leave you nor forsake you" (Deuteronomy 31:6).

If I could do ministry again I would have less fear and trust God to be true to His promise in my life.

2 ▶ I WOULD WATCH LESS TELEVISION AND FIND A MORE POSITIVE WAY TO "GEAR DOWN" AT THE END OF THE DAY

There are many things of which a wise man might wish to be ignorant.

—RALPH WALDO EMERSON

Most preachers are eager to totally relax late in the evening. I was no different. When I got home from a long day I was often physically and emotionally exhausted. I didn't want to read any more books, write any more articles, or talk to any more people. As a result, many nights from 9:30–11:00 I'd vegetate in front of the television set.

As you know, there's nothing like inane television programs to numb the mind and provide a semi-escape from the real world.

Around eleven I'd get drowsy and head up to bed and watch a half-hour of news on the TV set in the bedroom before falling asleep. Today technology has shifted this temptation from the television set to the smartphone. Where I found escape through television programs, the next generation withdraws from relationships and responsibility by staring at a much smaller screen that sucks them into a black hole of texting, tweets, and games. It's mesmerizing and limitless! I'm confident if that's your siren song you will have no trouble relating my battle with the remote control to your struggle with your iPhone.

Let's be realistic—we all need some downtime. There's nothing wrong with wanting to relax after working ten- to twelve-hour days. Our minds have been racing and we need to calm down. We've been in conversations all day—usually guarding our words, so it's normal to want to be quiet and not have to talk any more. We need some diversion, some time to wind down and de-stress.

However, looking back I realize now that I wasted so many hours watching meaningless ballgames, reruns of *Seinfeld*, or just channel surfing, searching for something that would captivate my attention. Admittedly, I sometimes wound up watching programs that I had no business watching, which subtly polluted my mind.

The Bible says that we're going to have to give account for every empty word that we speak (Matthew 12:36) and that "there is nothing hidden that will not be disclosed" (Luke 8:17). I dread standing before God and having to admit how much time I completely wasted in my lifetime staring at a television screen.

If I had spent just a half-hour less watching television each night for six nights a week, for the past fifty years I would have had a total of 7,800 hours for something more productive. That's the equivalent of 325 days . . . almost an entire year of life! That's just thirty minutes less a day! The truth is I could have cut out an hour most days—and not missed a thing. That's sad. I really regret that. At the very least I could have exercised while watching television but I didn't even do that.

If I could live my life again, I would discipline myself to do some recreational reading that would have broadened my mind. Or I could have taken up a meaningful hobby. I could have taken up painting, photography, cooking or learned to play our piano that was idle in the very next room instead of watching worthless television programs. I could have taken that time to listen to music CDs or books on audio.

I have a preacher friend who relaxes by spending several evenings each week doing woodworking projects in his garage. He learned the craft from scratch and is now very good at making furniture and meaningful items for his family. In a recent visit he gave me a gift of a wooden pen he'd made with his own hands. He's got something productive to do in retirement, whereas I am prepared to discuss *Andy Griffith* reruns or answer a sports trivia question. I'd like to turn back the clock to 9:30 each night so I could do something more productive with my leisure time.

"IDLE HANDS . . ."

When talking with pastors about this issue I point out it's really a lot more critical than just wasting time. There's an old saying, "Idle hands are the devil's workshop." King David discovered that. One year when he would normally go off to war David stayed home and strolled on the palace rooftop. It was at that point, when he was just lounging around, that he spotted Bathsheba bathing on the other side of the street. He looked. He lusted. He acted out. He suffered the consequences.

Our visibility as pastors makes it more of a temptation to go relax in front of the TV, happy in the privacy of our own homes.

TV can cleverly lead us into the world of darkness.

Ministers know we are being carefully observed nearly every minute in public. Our congregations and the local community are watching to see if our walk matches our talk. Whether it's driving our kids to school, buying items at the grocery store, sitting in the stands at Little League ballgames, attending a local concert, or standing in line at a movie theater, there is a sense in which we are onstage all the time. That's exhausting. But that high-profile position does give us some degree of accountability.

When we come home at night we're eager to relax and be totally comfortable—and isolated. The easiest way to chill out is to crash in the easy chair and pick up the remote and see what's on television. Television provides an instant escape from the difficulties and discouragements of ministry. Television is instant entertainment. Its producers are specialists in capturing and keeping our attention and so for a few minutes we forget the pressures and problems of the day.

Television is almost hypnotic. Its rapid changes eliminate the need to concentrate. I've read studies that show the average image on television changes in less than three seconds—so that the eye never rests. There's always something new to see. As a result there's no strain on the attention span. This constant stimulation of the senses through action and novelty eliminates the need to pay attention for more than a few seconds at a time.

But let's be honest: Television not only captures attention and provides an escape; it can cleverly lead us into the world of darkness. The bloody violence, frequent profanity, worldly propaganda, and graphic sexuality available on television does more than entertain, it can pollute our minds, desensitize us to evil, entice us to lust, quench the Holy Spirit in our lives, and dull the edge of our sword. For me, television was more dangerous than a computer. I've counseled with guys who have become addicted to Internet pornography. I know about its potential hazards so I have appropriate blockage on my home computer. I am also aware that people can trace where I've been on the Internet. In the event of an injury or death I don't want my wife or my children to see that I've been to inappropriate sites and disappoint them. So there's a sense in which there's more accountability on the computer and it's not a frequent temptation.

But no one can trace where we've been while channel surfing. In most instances there's little blockage on the television. In many cases we're sitting alone in front of the television. The lines of right and wrong are not as clearly defined. There are more grey areas and its temptations are more insidious.

"DO YOU WANT TO GET WELL?"

Since my experience is a common one for preachers let me suggest some positive action I would take if I had a do-over in this area. Hopefully it will help you make better use of your "downtime" than I did. I'm aware this chapter may not apply at all to some of you, but if you spend an hour or two in front of the television set every night let me offer some suggestions that are helping me in this final chapter of life. A few of these ideas may seem extreme to you but I ask you, as Jesus asked the man who had been disabled for thirty-eight years, "Do you want to get well?"

(1) I would not subscribe to any premium cable movie channels in my home.

Thankfully, I never did subscribe to Cinemax, Showtime, HBO, or the numerous cable movie channels that are offered. If you have subscribed, cancel them. You can rationalize that you need to watch *Game of Thrones* or other hip programs to stay abreast of the culture. But in reality you don't need that—you can read a synopsis and know what's going on.

These "premium" cable channels feature late-night programming that increasingly includes pornography that is too tempting for any man—no matter how spiritually strong he may think he is. In Deuteronomy 7:26, God warned the Israelites not to bring false idols into their homes, lest they be ensnared by it. He added, "Do not bring a detestable thing into your house or you, like it, will be set apart for destruction. Regard it as vile and utterly detest it, for it is set apart for destruction."

Although a television set isn't exactly an idol in the Old Testament sense, the graphic nudity, gross profanity, and anti-Christ worldview offered through premium cable channels is even more dangerous. We know down deep inside that those programs don't belong in a home that has a plaque on the wall that reads, "Jesus Christ is the head of this house. He's the unseen guest at every meal and the silent listener to every conversation."

A year ago my wife and I decided to change our cable provider for a variety of reasons. The installer for the new company informed us that as a bonus we would have all the movie channels for free for the first three months. I said, "No thanks, we'd just like basic cable." He said, "Well, we can install it for free for the first three months, then if you don't want it you can let us know."

I said, "No, please don't install it at all. I don't want that kind of raunchy programming available in our house." He said, "Sir, I understand, we've got children and grandchildren in our home too, and I don't want them to have access to those adult programs either so we block them." I said, "To be honest, I don't want them available for me—not just my grandchildren." He seemed somewhat puzzled and then a few minutes later said, "Sir, I'll not include the premium cable channels and, oh, by the way, there's a twenty-two-dollar discount if you choose not to have the free movie channels the first three months." Really!

I didn't just make a sound economic decision, but a good spiritual decision. It would have cost me too much in the way of daily temptation and family example to have those channels available in my house.

(2) I would use the Parental Blockage feature on my television to block all programs rated "R" and "M" and then throw away the access code.

Most R-rated movies are "edited for television" on network channels but frequently they are not edited enough, so it's wise to block them and throw away the four-digit code. You don't need them. If you remember the code, have your wife block it for you and she can throw away the record. (One of the advantages of being seventy-two years old is that I have no problem forgetting the code!)

*(3) I would be more intentional
about what programs I was going to watch.*

Too often I picked up the remote and thought, "Let's see what's on television tonight" and started channel surfing. It's wiser to look first at the program guide and make a selection and watch that one program exclusively.

*(4) I would use commercial
breaks to do something productive.*

I hate to watch the same vapid ads again and again, so I'm tempted to surf for two- or three-minute segments and actually take pride in the fact that I can watch two or three programs at once.

Instead of surfing during commercials it would be so much more productive to place a stack of thank-you cards in the drawer beside your favorite chair and when a three-minute series of ads comes on, take time to write someone a thank-you note or a sympathy card. Just a few sentences from the preacher will mean the world to some church member and you'll be amazed at how many cards you can write in the course of one basketball or football game.

If you're not a note-writer, keep your iPad by your side and send an email to a friend. There's no time-pressure and it takes little mental effort. You'll feel so much better when it's time to go to bed because you've accomplished something positive in your spare time.

*(5) I'd fast from watching any
television at least one night a week.*

I wouldn't be legalistic about this and I'd choose a night when there's not usually a meaningful program or an important game on that I wanted to watch, then determine not to turn the television on at all. Instead of looking for something to occupy my time I'd try talking to my wife or family members.

My wife and I had dinner on the back porch the other night. Afterward we sat and talked for an hour. It was amazing! We enjoyed each other's company and I gave her my total attention. That experience reminded me of an email someone sent me a few months ago.

"I had a power outage at my house this morning and my PC, laptop, TV, DVD, iPad, and my new surround-sound music system were all shut down. Then I discovered that my iPhone battery was flat. To top it off, it was raining so I couldn't go for a walk, bike, or run. The garage door opener needs electricity so I couldn't go anywhere in the car.

"I went into the kitchen to make coffee, and then I remembered that it also needed power . . . so I sat and talked with my wife for a few hours . . . She seems like a nice person."

That's funny! But it's also convicting. We can live under the same roof with people, even sleep in the same bed with them and actually not know them very well because we spend so little time in meaningful dialogue. We use electronic gadgets and travel privileges to escape from in-depth conversations.

Deep relationships take time and effort to develop. They are risky because they require making ourselves vulnerable and it's possible we could get hurt. So we often choose to take the easy way out and avoid them. We're more comfortable with surface conversations or text messages that we can terminate at any minute. Even at home we're more comfortable with the noise on the television set than the uncomfortable silence when the conversation lags.

*(6) I'd look for something positive
and edifying to do with my leisure time.*

As mentioned earlier, my son Rusty is the minister of a church in Port Charlotte, Florida. He and his wife, Kellie, have four children. They are intentional about eating their evening meal together, and no one is allowed to leave the table until they read a passage of Scripture and then pray for someone in the church who sent them a Christmas card. They keep all the cards they receive and discard them only after they have taken time to pray for the one who sent it.

But Rusty's family practices another positive habit. They play a lot of games as a family in the evenings. Instead of turning on the television and vegging out, someone will ask, "How about a game of Rummikub, Scrabble, Clue, or Monopoly? During those family times occasionally serious conversations develop, and it's a teaching and bonding time for the family. That doesn't happen when the television is on continuously.

*(7) I'd experiment with not having a television set in
our home for one year—especially with children at home.*

Admittedly, this would be a big sacrifice for me because I'm a sports junkie, and I really enjoy following University of Louisville football and basketball games. I look forward to the NCAA tournament and the college football bowl games. But most of the games are now available on the Internet, and I have friends with television sets! It's possible . . .

TAKING PHILIPPIANS 4:8 SERIOUSLY

Dr. Matthew Sleeth is a former emergency room physician and chief of staff at a New England hospital. Matt and his wife, Nancy, were dramatically converted to Christ a little over a decade ago. They left their affluent, hectic lifestyle on the coast of Maine and now dedicate their lives to leading others to the Lord. He's the founder of Blessed Earth Ministry, the author of 24-6,[1] and a popular speaker and lecturer.

Matthew has helped me look at the need for a weekly Sabbath and the importance of being a good steward of the earth's resources in a fresh way. Dr. Sleeth is one of those guys who sees truths in Scripture most of us have overlooked. He's a brilliant thinker who always challenges my thinking.

I am most impressed with how much Bible Matthew has learned in a relatively short period of time. He has a spiritual depth and love for Christ that I've not seen in many Christian leaders. I'm convinced one of the keys to his rapid spiritual growth is that he decided shortly after becoming a Christian to eliminate television from his home.

The Sleeths decided to take Philippians 4:8 seriously: "Whatever is true, whatever is noble, whatever is right, whatever is pure, whatever is lovely, whatever is admirable . . . think about such things." A part of that discipline was unplugging their family from cable television. He concluded that horror movies and raunchy sitcoms clutter his mind and that of his family.

"About the time I became a Christian, that phrase from Scripture, 'renewing your mind,' stuck in my head," Matthew said.

Instead of watching TV, he began to take courses in "The Great Courses" program. He has done "about a hundred."

I asked Dr. Sleeth, "What about the news? How do you keep abreast of what's going on in the world?" He responded that in his opinion most of us are way "over-newsed. People used to get all the news they needed in fifteen minutes at the end of the day . . . Now we're too much involved in the news. The twenty-four-hour news stations can suck you right in and do nothing for you. They

"It's better to watch a good movie three times than a bad movie once."

find ways to extend and exaggerate the day's events to improve ratings. Jesus said, 'Each day has enough trouble of its own' (Matthew 6:34). You can find out what's going on in the world by reading a newspaper about thirty minutes a week."

Dr. Sleeth told me, "My only experience with television now is when I'm in a hotel room. If I do flip on the television set, three hours will go by like I'm on crack cocaine. When the ads come on I start surfing and forget what show I'm watching." He came to the conclusion that it was best not to turn the television set on in the hotel room.

"I don't want that stuff in my brain," he said. "I believe that Paul is telling us to fill ourselves with light. 'What partnership does light have with darkness?' It doesn't—all you get is gray. Our family is also much more intentional about what movies we watch. It's better to watch a good movie three times than a bad movie once. So much of what you see on television desensitizes you to Satan's world.

"I wonder if many of today's youth have the same problem with social media and video games?" Dr. Sleeth asked. "I suspect that sitting for hours in front of a screen is a gateway drug to pornography. We're too accustomed to being mesmerized and entertained by the action on the screen."

Matthew and Nancy have developed a good habit of reading to each other out loud when they travel or when they are at home together at night. They read aloud to their children from *The Chronicles of Narnia* and *Mere Christianity*, and now that their kids are grown they still often get together on Friday nights and read aloud to one another.

> *I'll never forget my godly mother getting out of her chair, stalking to the TV, and nearly snapping the knob off.*

That's helpful! Taking into your mind only what is wholesome. Visiting with your family. Reading aloud to one another. Developing your thinking through ongoing education. It's so basic, how can we miss it? But it all begins with the simple discipline of turning off the television and finding something else to do.

I remember as a young boy when our family got our first television set. I was in the sixth grade and we were thrilled. One evening we were all watching a program in which a man and woman shared a passionate kiss. It was probably very mild by today's standards, but it made everyone in the family uncomfortable in that day. There we sat glued to the television, no one saying a word. This was in the mid-fifties, long before the remote control, but I'll never forget my godly mother getting up out of her chair, stalking across the room, and nearly snapping the knob off. She turned and said tersely, "Let's talk." Everyone started jabbering immediately, pretending like we hadn't been paying much attention to what was on the screen. I wish I had followed my mother's example the rest of my life. I think I would have been a more Spirit-filled preacher.

"Be very careful, then, how you live—not as unwise but as wise, making the most of every opportunity, because the days are evil" (Ephesians 5:15–16).

3 ▶ I'D PAY LESS ATTENTION TO CRITICISM AND GIVE MORE ATTENTION TO SWIMMING WITH THE FISH

You can't let praise or criticism get to you. It's a weakness to get caught up in either one.

—JOHN WOODEN

All leaders are sensitive to criticism. Publicly they talk a good game about "rising above negativity," but the truth is, criticism hurts. Whether it's in the form of a vicious anonymous letter, a snide remark, or a sarcastic public comment, most leaders chafe under the sting of criticism. Criticism is like a battering ram; externally it doesn't appear to do any damage at first but it wears down the internal structure until we eventually cave in.

As our church grew and my ministry expanded through radio programs and Christian publications, I became a frequent target of criticism. It got so I was criticized on the average of once a day.

"We want something deeper than you're providing on Wednesday night."

"We don't like the music so we're considering going elsewhere."

"That article you wrote about Pentecost put God in a box. You need to think deeper thoughts about what God can do in the church."

One Sunday morning a woman stopped me in the hallway between services and said, "Brother Russell, I was so disappointed you recommended in your sermon today that people go see the movie, *The Chronicles of Narnia*." "Why is that?" I asked.

"Because it's got witchcraft in it!" she chirped.

I asked, "Did you see the movie?"

"No, I wouldn't go see it because I know it's got witchcraft in it."

"Did you read C. S. Lewis's books The Chronicles of Narnia?"

"No, it's got witchcraft in it!"

I responded with some degree of exasperation, "So does the Bible. But it's against it. Do you read it?"

People!

WHEN YOU CAN'T WIN . . .

Sometimes people thought they were encouraging me when their comments were actually hurtful. Toward the end of my ministry a member flippantly told me, "We really liked that sermon you preached last Sunday; it was more like the ones you used to preach when we first came here." Somehow that didn't build me up much.

People thought I didn't preach enough on prayer, the Holy Spirit, prophecy, or abortion. I neglected to mention single mothers on Mother's Day. I failed to mention a missionary who requested prayer. I called the auditorium a sanctuary and that was not the correct New Testament term. I wrote *complemented* and it should have been spelled *complimented*. I quoted Dr. Schuller and he's liberal; I quoted Dr. Laura and she's rude. On and on it goes!

In a sermon to our brotherhood's National Convention I spoke about our need to include believers from other groups as our brothers and sisters in Christ. In that sermon I said, "Since we're going to spend eternity with Billy Graham, James Dobson, Chuck Colson, Bill Gaither, and Charles Swindoll, I'd like to get to know them on earth."

I knew that would rankle a few in our movement who were very sectarian and narrow-minded—the very opposite of what the Christian Church was intended to be. But I didn't anticipate how strong the opposition would be. I got sixteen critical letters accusing me of denying the faith once and for all delivered to the saints. (It's sad that I even took the time to count the letters. That's an indication that I let criticism bother me too much.)

One brotherhood preacher at a large family convention shortly afterward barked, "We have this preacher down in Louisville who thinks he's going to spend eternity with Dobson, Colson, Swindoll, and the Gaithers. He may spend eternity with them but it won't be in heaven!"

The criticism that hurt the most was that which had just enough truth in it to sting.

To be honest, that kind of criticism didn't bother me nearly as much since it came from outside the local church. The criticism that hurt most was that which came from within, from people I loved . . . and that had just enough truth in it to sting.

Anytime I dared preach on stewardship I knew I was inviting criticism. I didn't preach on money very often but one series a year was too often for some people. No matter what approach you take, regardless of how much Scripture or humor you use, there will always be some who don't want to hear what the Bible says about money. It's just a sensitive subject and people are offended . . . or they feel guilty.

Invariably someone will say, "I've worked for months to get my friends to come to church and the first time they came you preached about money. I told them that doesn't happen very often but I doubt they'll ever come back." Or, "You preachers have a one-track mind. You're always looking for some angle to get into our pocketbooks."

In one fund-raising campaign we mailed out a brochure, asking every member and participant to make a generous commitment. I received the following anonymous letter. "Dear Bob Russell, At a time in all our lives when our State and our County is experiencing a totally unstable economy, services cut for the most needy individuals, you have the gall to ask for 30 million dollars from the Southeast Community. May God help you in your greed. If you raise 30 million dollars, give it to the State of Kentucky, not so Bob Russell can pat himself on the back, 'See what I have done now! I'm the greatest.' What was the cost associated with printing and mailing this outrageous brochure!" Of course he/she didn't sign their name.

That's just one of several mean-spirited anonymous letters I received during that campaign. It was about that time that I told the secretary who opened my mail to discard all anonymous letters. If people don't have enough courage to sign their name they forfeit the opportunity to disturb my mood.

Some people keep all the encouraging letters they receive, and I kept a number of positive notes. But for years I kept almost all

Guys say, "It makes me feel so much better to know I'm not the only one being attacked."

my critical letters. One reason is I'm able to look back on them a year or two later and I can usually see how ridiculous they were. That helps me not to get so upset over current negative letters. Another reason is that somehow my critical letters encourage other preachers! Guys say, "It makes me feel so much better to know I'm not the only one who gets attacked."

Once I got a letter asking me to publicly announce that we were disassociating from the Southland Christian Church in Lexington because they had decided not to have services when Christmas Day fell on Sunday. A national article reported that Southland and other megachurches were encouraging their people to come to the Christmas Eve services and spend Sunday with their families or in Christian service.

We had exchanged pulpits and programs with Southland in the past, but now one of our people wanted me to publicly announce we had cut off our relationship with them because they were taking a lot of heat from the press for not having services on Christmas Day. Really?

Our elders considered doing the same thing. But we finally concluded there would probably be a few people who could not attend the Christmas Eve service and could only come on Sunday morning, so we would have a service on Sunday. We would make it simple and devotional in nature. Someone suggested we wouldn't need two services and also suggested instead of meeting in the large auditorium we meet in the fellowship hall and the setting would be more intimate. That's what we did and the service was actually very inspirational.

But wouldn't you know, an older couple came that morning and went directly into the darkened sanctuary and sat there the entire hour. Greeters came in and whispered, "We're meeting in the fellowship hall." With tears in their eyes the older couple responded, "Yes, we're aware of that. But we think this is where the Lord intends His people to be on the Lord's Day."

And people asked me why I retired!

I know what's going to happen. The next time Christmas falls on Sunday the elders will discuss what to do. Someone will suggest, "Let's do like we did last time and have a worship service in the fellowship hall." I can almost guarantee you someone will say, "Well, maybe we shouldn't do that. Remember last time we got 'a lot' of criticism. Some people weren't real happy with that decision."

We often allow a small handful of vocal critics to manipulate us and prevent us from making decisions that are best for the vast majority. When we face decisions we need to ask two questions. First, what does God want us to do? (What will be the best thing for our church in five years?) Second, we need to ask, how will people respond? That's important too because we shouldn't bulldoze over people's feelings. But if question number two ever becomes more important than question number one, we sign the death warrant of our church.

LETTING IT GET TO YOU

Looking back I realize that I allowed criticism to bother me far more than it should have. I pretended not to. But I confess I allowed a few negative comments to sour my mood for days and rob me of my joy. I churned about it. I allowed it to affect my mood at home. I griped about it with friends and sometimes backed off programs or messages because I just didn't want to hear it again. Solomon spoke of "little foxes that ruin the vineyards" (Song of Solomon 2:15), and I let the little critical varmints spoil my spirit too often. I wish now I had not exaggerated its significance.

Max Lucado was a guest speaker for us one weekend, and it just so happened to be on the heels of a very unpleasant conversation I had with a church member. The husband of a woman who felt I had treated her unfairly had asked to have breakfast with me. If I'm the CEO of a company I don't have breakfast with the spouse of a disgruntled employee. But I'm not a CEO; I'm the pastor of a church. I liked this couple. I wanted this family to remain in the church and move forward.

But when I met this seething husband for breakfast at 7:30 in the morning he was accompanied by his wife. I knew what he was going to do. He was going to grandstand for her and chew me out in front of her for not being more supportive. He was going to find fault with the church and tell me how she would never have been treated so poorly in the business world.

I decided that it was futile to try to answer each of his criticisms. For every explanation there would be a counter-answer, and it would prolong the pain. Then I'd have to respond to letters from their friends and supporters asking me to defend some out-of-context quote.

So I made a choice to do what Muhammad Ali did in his 1974 bout with George Foreman in Zaire. In what is known as "The Rumble in the Jungle," Ali went into his famous "rope-a-dope." He just covered his head with his gloves and allowed Foreman to pound away until he was exhausted.

This couple pounded away on me for about an hour, and I walked away without retaliating. But I was exhausted . . . and angry. I am a competitor and I had not vented. Max Lucado and I played golf a few hours later. I turned on a shot and watched as my ball hooked abruptly and went over a dam into a lake. I said, "Max, did that ball go over the dam into the water?" He said, "Yes it did." I said, "I knew it did. I just wanted to say 'dam.'"

Now, I don't curse. But I admit, sometimes I want to. That earlier criticism was dragging me down in attitude and thought. The bad thing about it was Max got into the pulpit that weekend and told the congregation what I'd said! They had known me for a long time and didn't seem too shocked by it.

I'd like to turn back the clock and laugh at some of the criticism that seemed so disturbing at the time but was of so little consequence later.

> *The couple pounded away on me for about an hour and I walked away without retaliating. But I was exhausted.*

If I had a do-over in ministry, I'd try harder to obey the command of Jesus, "Blessed are you when people insult you, persecute you and falsely say all kinds of evil against you because of me. Rejoice and be glad, because great is your reward in heaven, for in the same way they persecuted the prophets who were before you" (Matthew 5:11–12).

COPING WITH CRITICISM

However unpleasant, effective leaders must learn to live with the criticism. Someone said, "If you're going to carry the ball, you're going to get tackled." If you're going to lead, you're going to be attacked. The Bible says, "Consider him who endured such opposition from sinners, so that you will not grow weary and lose heart" (Hebrews 12:3). Nobody received more vicious or frequent criticism than Jesus—yet He didn't quit. And, "In your struggle against sin, you have not yet resisted to the point of shedding your blood" (Hebrews 12:4). So don't grow weary and lose heart.

Criticism of leaders is nothing new. Over 2,500 years ago the prophet Nehemiah was doing an effective job of rebuilding the broken-down walls of Jerusalem. His determined team was on schedule to complete the task in less time than expected. He had enthusiastic support from the vast majority of his people.

But Nehemiah was also the target of vicious criticism. Two local residents, Sanballat and Tobiah, despised the Jews and made fun of the wall. "Even a fox could knock it over," they scoffed. When Nehemiah refused to be intimidated or distracted by their ridicule, Sanballat and Tobiah wrote him a letter expressing their displeasure and requested a meeting to discuss their objections.

Nehemiah's response was classic. He basically said, "I'm doing an important work and I don't have time to hear your gripes." That wasn't cocky—it was smart. It wasn't flippant—it was the wisest use of his time.

As I've shared, I had to learn to cope with criticism. In my younger years any disagreement really discouraged me. Friends and family spent considerable energy nursing my wounded ego. But eventually experience and Scripture helped me cope with criticism more effectively.

Perhaps some younger Christian leaders can benefit from some of the lessons I learned.

Remember all effective leaders are criticized. If you are on the front lines of battle, you're probably going to get shot at. It's that simple. We are involved in an intensifying spiritual war and the enemy is becoming increasingly malicious and mean-spirited. One gets the impression that if the world can just prove enough Christians are phony then they'll feel vindicated in their unbelief.

If you dare to speak God's truth or attempt to lead God's people, you are going to be attacked as a hatemonger, hypocrite, or a fool. Expect it and toughen up. Oswald Sanders, in his classic book *Spiritual Leadership*, suggests maturity is moving from a thin skin and hard heart to a soft heart and tough skin.[1]

Consider the source. Is it a petty, small-minded person who is griping or someone you respect? If it's from someone you hold in high regard, evaluate it carefully.

If you're on the front lines of battle, you're probably going to get shot at.

Maybe the Lord is using them to point out a blind spot in your life or your work. However, if the criticism comes from a puny-minded

Sanballat or Tobiah, then it's not worth the time and effort to answer it.

Evaluate the objection. If the criticism has some validity, then receive it with grace and make the necessary adjustment. If it doesn't, then ignore it and move on. I almost never answer a mean-spirited criticism. I conclude the critic is too angry to listen to reason. They just want to vent. It's a waste of time to answer grossly untrue criticisms, and it usually gives more validity to the objection than it merits.

Keep your focus on the ultimate goal. Don't mumble and grumble about the critics. That takes your mind off your primary responsibility. Don't let Satan distract you from what needs to get done. Your assignment is to please Christ, not men. His is the only opinion that ultimately matters. People are so fickle. The same people who criticize you today may be singing your praises tomorrow.

Find a way to get it off your mind. If I can't get a criticism off my mind and it's affecting my mood or distracting me, I will type out exactly what I'd like to say without any concern about being kind. However, I don't mail that unguarded communication immediately. I wait a day or two and never wind up mailing it in its original form—and seldom mail it at all. But by venting my feelings in a letter I get them out of my mind and onto the computer screen. Then it's easier to forget it and refocus on the task at hand.

Get bolder. The temptation is to become timid and avoid controversy altogether. That's what the enemy wants! But Jesus warned, "If anyone is ashamed of me and my message, the Son of Man will be ashamed of that person when he returns in his glory" (Luke 9:26 NLT). Don't let the enemy's bullying tactics intimidate you. Speak the truth in love, but speak the truth. King David urged, "Let the redeemed of the Lord say so" (Psalm 107:2 KJV).

The first-century Christians were threatened with imprisonment and death if they continued to speak about the resurrected Jesus in public. They didn't retreat or get more cautious. They prayed, "Now, Lord, consider their threats and enable your servants to speak your word with great boldness . . . And they were all filled with the Holy Spirit and spoke the word of God boldly" (Acts 4:29, 31).

Give God thanks for persecution. Jesus urged us when persecuted to "rejoice and be glad, because great is your reward in heaven" (Matthew 5:11–12). When we can praise God and be thankful for criticism, then we know we are growing in spiritual maturity and following in the footsteps of prophets like Nehemiah. That's pretty good company.

SWIM WITH THE FISH!

If I could do ministry again, I would pay less attention to unreasonable criticism but I would be more aggressive in seeking objective feedback.

King Solomon wrote, "Plans fail for lack of counsel, but with many advisers they succeed" (Proverbs 15:22). Preachers get so gun-shy about receiving negative comments that we subconsciously isolate ourselves from people whose input could be a tremendous help. As a result we lose touch and make unwise choices.

Now that I'm retired, once a month I take a mentoring group consisting of eight preachers to the Louisville Slugger Museum— the number one tourist attraction in Louisville. After a tour of the bat factory, Jack Hillerich, the owner, and Bill Clark, the president, spend time with the young ministers discussing leadership. One of the core values of Louisville Slugger is "Swim with the Fish."

Bill Clark places a fishbowl in the center of the conference table and points out that the fish represent their baseball players, retail merchants, salesman, suppliers, and factory workers—all the people they do business with on a regular basis. He insists most leadership teams are guilty of making "four-wall decisions." They look at the fish in the bowl and conclude, "We know our fish. We've specialized in fish for decades. We know what the fish need." Then they make decisions in the four walls of the boardroom on behalf of the fish. He adds, "When we make four-wall decisions, my observation is that 90 percent of the time we're wrong. We think we know our fish but we really don't know them. And we waste a lot of time and money trying to recover."

Bill says for decisions to be most effective, the leaders need to jump into the fishbowl and swim with the fish for a period of time. "We discover after swimming with the fish that 90 percent of the time we make right decisions."

Clark cites an example of the company leaders discussing how to market a new golf glove. Someone on the leadership team suggested they package the innovative glove in a box that resembled the new iPhone package that everyone thought was so cool. That would be different, it would be cutting edge and it was sure to get attention. Everyone agreed.

The company spent thousands of dollars in packaging and marketing only to discover the glove, though a peerless product, was not selling at all. Someone pointed out, "We forgot to swim with the fish." So they went to several golf shops and asked the owners, "Why isn't this glove selling?" At the very first stop, the golf pro said, "That's easy. People don't even know it's a golf glove.

It's very confusing to the customer. If people figure it out, they don't know how to open it. Then if they do open it, they can't try the glove on and then the glove ends up on the floor and not back in the package. No wonder it doesn't sell. It's the worst packaging I've ever seen."

Hillerich & Bradsby executives then went back to the drawing board, swam with their fish (golfers), and then completely redesigned the package to appeal to the consumer rather than jumping at the latest hip idea offered by a junior vice president in a boardroom.

The application to the local church is obvious. As the church grows or as a minister remains with a congregation for a few years, there is a tendency to swim with the fish less and make more and more four-wall decisions. After all, we have been there before. We know our people. Why waste time swimming with the fish? Why give them a chance to gripe? Our staff members are trained in seminary. They've been to leadership seminars. They have creative ideas. As a result we dump top-down programs on the congregation that are ill suited or ill timed and months later we wind up trying to analyze what went wrong.

Take the typical youth department, for example. Who designs and evaluates the annual youth retreat? Usually the youth minister, who is often gifted at winging it, plans the youth retreat three or four days in advance. When the retreat is over everyone says, "We had fun" and nothing is done about next year's retreat until the week before when the student minister repeats the same mediocre cycle.

What if the student minister swam with the fish? What if after the retreat he gathered a handful of the teenagers and their parents and asked open-ended questions about how the retreat could be improved and jotted down the suggestions? If the youth staff planned next year's retreat with those suggestions in mind, I guarantee you it would improve annually.

Who evaluates a worship service? Usually the worship team gets together afterward and they ask each other, "How do you think it went?" The answers are subjective and from the perspective of those on the platform. Keep in mind the musicians have rehearsed the praise songs and sung them dozens of times before the congregation has even heard them once. They tire of a song long before the congregation does. Keep in mind they are all excellent musicians who love to sing and have a wide range of musical talent, unlike the average person in the church who isn't a gifted singer and who struggles to hit the high notes. The four-wall thinking of the worship staff is often way out of touch with the person in the pew.

What if the worship team took time to swim with the fish? On a day they're not onstage, they sit in a different seat and listen to the singing and the comments of the fish. What if they took a practical survey of the types of worship songs that the congregation prefers to sing? What if they simply asked, "What really draws you closer to God during worship?" Or, "What would you like to see happen more often in our service?" I suspect worship services would be considerably different . . . and more impactful.

The four-wall thinking of the worship staff is often way out of touch with the person in the pew.

Many are afraid to provide that venue because it opens the door to complaints. But as Jack Hillerich and Bill Clark point out, we need to listen to even the disgruntled fish. Sometimes they have positive suggestions.

Sometimes if leadership gives them an ear, they are less likely to complain to others in the congregation. In an article entitled "Service Is King," Danny Meyer, creator of New York's Union Square Café and other popular restaurants, suggests, "The customer is not always right, but the customer wants to be heard."[2]

The same principle applies to preaching. If I had ministry to do over, I would find more ways to get feedback from the congregation and not just rely on suggestions from family or staff people. Once when I did a series on divorce and remarriage, I invited five divorced couples to meet with me in the office after the Wednesday evening service to discuss my upcoming sermon.

On another occasion I had a sermon on improving race relations and invited six African American members to meet with me to discuss the subject. Both times I benefited from the input of the congregation, and those who met with me were my biggest advocates. In hindsight I should have done that kind of thing more often. But it was easier just to discuss it for a few minutes with associate ministers because they were more available.

I made the mistake at times of giving too much credence to critical comments from people who didn't matter and didn't spend enough time swimming with the fish who really did matter. If I could do it again, I would be more intentional about gaining feedback from mature people in the congregation through focus groups, brief surveys, and open discussions. I'm convinced I would have benefited a great deal from their input.

4 ▶ I'D BE KINDER, MORE ATTENTIVE, AND MORE ANIMATED WITH MY WIFE

*Let the wife make the husband glad to come home,
and let him make her sorry to see him leave.*

—MARTIN LUTHER

In the first few years of marriage I was not a great husband. I wasn't horrible, but I was far from the best I could be. After one year of marriage I accepted the call to minister to the Southeast Christian Church in Louisville, Kentucky. I knew I was in way over my head and needed to work hard and be totally focused for this new, challenging ministry.

Often when we went to church for worship I forgot about Judy until it was time to go home. Then sometimes I would ask her to wait in the car while I counseled someone who really needed me at the last moment. I allowed phone calls to interrupt family time at home. I was gone for several hours most nights attending meetings or making home visits.

Probably my biggest mistake was that when I was home I wasn't really home. When I came home at the end of the day, I was often tense and exhausted. I didn't want to talk. I just wanted to sit in the easy chair, read the paper, and take a nap. Then when we did get into what could be a meaningful conversation, my wife often received tepid attention and curt answers. My nose was often stuck in a book I needed to read for the upcoming sermon.

When two sons were added to our family, I started doing a little better about being at home for meals and bedtime. I'd heard the horror stories about preachers' kids going spiritually AWOL— sometimes because of neglect, so I gave attention to my boys. But my wife was still taken for granted. I knew she would always be there. And thankfully, she was. I owe her a huge debt because in those early days when she was lonely, she didn't complain or stray.

A WAKE-UP CALL

But after about a decade of being a halfhearted husband, one afternoon I got a phone call from Judy telling me that she was going to be home a little later than usual. I answered the phone so late that the answering machine kicked on and recorded our conversation without me knowing it. About twenty minutes later I saw the red light indicating there was a voice mail message so I pushed the button and listened to my response to her call.

I couldn't get over the contrast between the vitality and energy in Judy's voice and the deadness and disconnect in mine. "Bob, you having a good day?" "*Okay.*" "What are you doing?" "*Reading the paper.*" "Well, I just called to tell you that I got hung up a little at work and I'm going to be a little late. I'm sorry." "*Okay.*" "Do you want me to bring something home to eat or do you want to go out and get something together?" *"Doesn't matter."*

If that had been the average member of the church, I know my responses would have been so much more animated. "Are you having a good day?" "Yes! It's a great day! Thanks. Are you doing okay?"

"What are you doing?" "I'm reading the newspaper. Reading this article about UL's football team. Have you read that?"

"Just called to tell you I'm going to be late getting home. Do you want me to bring something or go out to eat?" "It doesn't matter. Just be careful. Don't hurry. Wouldn't want you to get into an accident . . . How about let's just eat here at the house so our conversation won't be interrupted?"

That's the way I would have responded to an average church member. But to my wife, the person who actually matters the most, my responses were mere grunts: okay, yeah, doesn't matter. Deep down I knew this wasn't just a onetime conversation.

Why do the people who matter the most get the least amount of our energy and attention?

That was a general practice. And I was convicted.

I had just read a book by Bruce Larson that had a chapter entitled "Are You Fun to Live With?"[1] I realized as I listened to that recording that I wasn't fun to live with! If I die, I want Judy to shed at least one tear! But at the time I wasn't sure she had any reason to weep.

Why is it the people we love the most we treat the worst? Why do the people who matter most get the least amount of our energy and attention? I vowed that day that I was going to change. That meant when I came home I was going to shift gears. Even though I was tired, I would make the effort to be more animated and fun-loving at home.

I intentionally made an adjustment. From that point on I quit bringing work home. When I walked away from my office around 5 p.m. I'd say, "Lord, that's the best I can do today. There are emails that need answering and phone calls to return and a sermon that's incomplete but those things will have to wait until tomorrow. This day's work is over."

As a result my evenings became more focused on the family and my marriage relationship made a giant step of improvement. Judy and I have laughed more, talked more, and have become much closer during the last period of our marriage than the first. I'm thankful my wake-up call came in an innocuous way, but I still wish I could have learned my lesson earlier.

Ben Merold, a much-admired preacher in the Christian Church, says wherever he lived he pounded a nail in the front door to the house. Some thought that nail was to hang notes or hats. But he said it served as a symbol to him every night. "That's where I would mentally hang all the 'junk' that's gone on during the day and I leave it outside when I walk into the house." Maybe that helps explain why he and his wife, Pat, have been happily married in a joint ministry for sixty-six years!

One Sunday evening after church Judy and I were eating pizza with the senior high youth in the church kitchen. She looked particularly attractive to me that evening, so I looked across the table at her and winked. She turned away like she was embarrassed. A couple hours later I was sitting in the recliner in the family room and she came up behind me and grabbed me around the neck and kissed me on the back of the neck. She murmured, "Do you know what that does to me when you wink at me in public?" I didn't. But I found out and decided I would do it again!

I regret not being a better husband over the first decade. I wish I would have winked at her and laughed with her more often. I know now that she sometimes felt lonely and neglected when I paid a lot more attention to others than I did her. I wish I could turn back the clock and have a do-over.

A DRAMATIC REMINDER

About twenty years ago Judy experienced a serious stroke. She had an irregular heartbeat that kicked out a small blood clot to her brain. I'm so thankful that God answered our prayers and she has totally recovered with the only after-effect being a little numbness in one hand. That numbness has limited her ability to play the piano, which was always a passion, but she says that's a small price to pay in light of what could have been.

However, the first two weeks after her stroke were touch-and-go. The first night in the hospital she cried out to me about one in the morning that something was drastically wrong, and suddenly she had a horrible seizure. Her lovely face and body just began twitching uncontrollably. I'd never seen anything like it, and we were terrified. We both thought she was having a second, massive stroke. I grabbed her hand and we pleaded for God's help. The nurses rushed into the room and explained what was happening and helped relieve some of our anxiety when it was over.

Twice more during that first night Judy had disturbing seizures. Antiseizure medicine proved helpful but then Judy had a horrible reaction to that medicine and began to weaken. Doctors were uncertain about the next course of action over the next few days and she appeared to grow weaker and weaker. It was a frightening and uncertain time for me.

Looking back, it seems providential that one week after her stroke, I was scheduled to preach at our brotherhood's annual convention. We were meeting in the RCA Dome in Indianapolis, and I was to address the opening night session where we were anticipating 40,000 people.

Most preachers would consider that a terrific honor and a highlight of their career. The night before the convention began I was sitting in the hospital room with Judy and didn't know whether I would preach at the convention or not—and I didn't much care. Judy rallied, insisted I go, and a friend drove me to Indianapolis. I preached the sermon and returned the same night. Somehow that speaking engagement didn't seem nearly as important as it would have otherwise.

I was reminded that we often don't appreciate someone until they are gone or we nearly lose them. Judy and I are both thankful that God has answered our prayers and granted us excellent health for the past twenty years. All of us need to remember that long after our kids have moved on, our ministries have concluded, and the elders have nearly forgotten our names, chances are good our wives will still be there. They merit focused attention and total devotion.

TAKE HEED!

It seems hardly a month goes by that we don't learn about another high-profile minister falling to gross moral failure. And statistics vary, but we all know pastors' homes that have been torn by divorce. We preach about the sanctity of marriage . . . but how can we "walk the talk"?

In discussing this issue with preachers and realistically evaluating my own temptations, I've come to several conclusions.

(1) Most preachers would be wise to eliminate marital counseling. The majority of moral failures can be traced back to intimate conversations that surfaced while discussing marriage problems. The initial temptation is usually more ego driven than sexually driven. It's not physical attraction but emotional identification that plants the seeds for an affair.

It just isn't wise to spend too much time alone with a member of the opposite sex who is not your married partner. It's even more foolish to discuss intimate subjects since most of us are not adequately trained for in-depth counseling. We can rationalize that biblical instruction is needed, but we're not the only ones capable of sharing God's Word. The best word I ever learned was "referral." It was a good day when I could say, "I don't do any marital counseling, but here's the name of a Christian psychologist I have confidence in. He can help you."

(2) Having a good marriage does not exempt you from temptation. We mistakenly conclude that since we are happily married we are immune from moral failure. In his book *Rebuilding Your Broken World*,[2] Gordon MacDonald quotes Oswald Chambers: "An unguarded strength can become a double weakness." And the Bible warns, "Therefore let anyone who thinks that he stands take heed lest he fall" (1 Corinthians 10:12 ESV). It's not as difficult to fall as we suppose.

(3) The surest way to overcome a fierce temptation is to confess

it to a trusted friend other than your mate. There's great wisdom in the advice of James 5:16, "Confess your sins to each other and pray for each other so that you may be healed."

(4) God can bless the ministry of imperfect people. I'm thankful that I never had an affair, but I

> *The best word I ever learned was "referral."*

would have to confess that there were times my heart wasn't as pure as it should have been.

If you've fallen to lustful and inappropriate thoughts, you need to repent and return to service. Don't let Satan convince you that you shouldn't be in ministry because you've allowed a flirtatious conversation to continue or you've wandered into an inappropriate website. Those are serious sins that could jeopardize your testimony and should be confronted and overcome. But they shouldn't be excuses to quit the ministry. God uses imperfect people; that's the only kind He has. Understand your high calling, repent of your sin, put on the full armor of God, and go to war on the frontlines of this intensifying spiritual battle. We need you!

(5) The blessings of victory far exceed the pleasures of sin. My happiest times in life today are those special occasions when I am with my wife, my two sons, my daughters-in-law, and my seven grandchildren. When we're all together laughing and enjoying one other I often think of that verse in 3 John 4, "I have no greater joy than to hear that my children are walking in the truth."

Dr. Lewis Foster, a beloved seminary professor of mine often repeated this wise saying, "Good though done with toil, the toil soon passes, but the good long will remain. Evil though done with pleasure, the pleasure soon passes, but the evil long will remain."

"ENJOYMENT, NOT JUST ENDURANCE"

Maybe instead of spending time lamenting preachers who have experienced a disappointing moral failure we need to celebrate those who have modeled faithfulness. I earlier mentioned Ben and Pat Merold, who have been married for sixty-six years. Ben insists, "I'm not half done with her yet!" Their love and respect for each other has been an inspiration to their church members and younger church leaders for decades. I've seen them at conventions walking hand in hand down the hallway many times. And I've watched other convention attendees nudge each other and point to Ben and Pat and smile. Inside we are all thinking, "That's what I want for my marriage when I get older."

Pat Merold was struck down with an aneurysm on her brain two weeks ago as I write this. She was rushed to the hospital and has been left with limited speech and mobility. When I called Ben he told me the doctors informed him it's going to be a long, slow healing process. "I'm on my way to the hospital right now," Ben, who is eighty-nine years old, said. "I'm taking her to rehab today. If anyone can make it, Pat can. She's a strong woman, you know." Inside I was thinking, "I've only been married for fifty years. That's what I want for my marriage when Judy and I get older!"

A year ago our sons said, "Mom and Dad, we know your fiftieth anniversary is coming up so we've reserved the Fireside Room at church to have a big celebration with friends." Several days later I responded, "Thanks for thinking of us and planning in advance. But to be honest, when we're the happiest is not when we're standing in line shaking hands and making small talk with hundreds of people. When we're the happiest is when we're with our family.

Instead of having an elaborate reception at church, why don't we just celebrate together as a family? Remember that time years ago when all thirteen of us stayed in Ronnie and Patricia Williams's cabin by the river in the Smoky Mountains? Let's do that again!" When I offered to pay for it, they were all in!

So the week of May 29, 2015, our family met at the Williams's cabin in Townsend, Tennessee. Everyone had such a great time tubing on the river, fishing for trout, riding horseback, playing golf, playing Monopoly, playing touch football, and cooking out. On Sunday morning we had our own worship service at the cabin. My grandson Charlie, who is in Bible college studying to be a worship leader, led worship, and his dad preached. My daughter-in-law Kellie sang and my grandchildren served Communion.

At the end of our in-home worship service I read the following tribute to my wife. I entitled it "Fifty Years of Marriage— Enjoyment, Not Just Endurance."

Fifty years ago this past Friday I stood in front of a little country church in Ohio and made a vow to be faithful to Judy Kay Thomas until we were separated by death.

There are tremendous advantages to being married to the same person for fifty years. You can relax and enjoy each other's company without having to entertain each other. You can be confident that you are the most important person in existence to at least one other person in the world. There's the security of knowing there's someone who knows everything about you and still loves you anyway.

Some people congratulate couples on their golden anniversary as if they've just won an endurance contest: "Wow! You've managed to stick it out for fifty years!" Every marriage has some rough spots, and ours is no exception, but I'm thankful that Judy and I have not just endured fifty years, we've enjoyed our time together and we can't imagine it being any other way.

As a tribute to my wife I'd like to list the top ten reasons why she's been easy to love and enjoyable to be with. I apologize for the length of this piece but there's a lot to be thankful for!

1. *Family heritage*—Both our parents were happily married for more than fifty years. That set the standard for what we both wanted our home to be.

2. *Mutual faith*—No matter how good a marriage is, sometimes you don't like each other very much and you stay together for the sake of Christ. The commitment to obey God's Word eliminates any consideration of divorce and motivates reconciliation. "If I'm going to live with this person the rest of my life, I'd better work this out or I've got a tough life ahead" is a lot different attitude than "If you don't change I'm leaving!"

3. *Even temperament*—Judy has a steady personality. She's like Jesus: "the same yesterday, today and forever." My personality fluctuates more than hers, but I always knew what she would be like when I came home. The one quality most young men underestimate in looking for a wife may be "Is she easy to live with?"

4. *Low maintenance*—My wife has never demanded a lot of attention. She is not easily wounded. She doesn't overspend. I've never known her to fake a tear. She's not into theatrics or melodrama in order to be noticed.

5. *Attractive appearance*—Judy was pretty when I married her, and she has continued to care for her appearance. I really appreciate that. It's inevitable that we both change. We gain weight, lose hair, and earn some wrinkles, but my wife is still attractive to me after five decades. I now love her for who she is on the inside but I still like the outside too!

6. *Frequent affection*—Of the five love languages listed by author Gary Chapman, Judy's is physical touch. She would rather I gently pat her on the face than buy her expensive gifts (with a few exceptions!). That need is easy to satisfy and saves a lot of money. Her consistent, warm responsiveness to me also eliminates temptation and makes me eager to come home.

7. *Needed space*—She doesn't "smother me" with love. We'd often go our separate ways at church and say, "Meet you at the end of the second service." Sometimes I go on speaking engagements and golf trips, and she occasionally takes short trips with friends or spends the day with her own interests. I think that's healthy. The old adage holds true for a long marriage: "Absence makes the heart grow fonder."

8. *Realistic expectations*—A lot of marriages struggle because of unrealistic fantasies. Couples who expect everyday romance and constant pampering discover those images are impossible to live up to. I think many ministers' marriages fail because the wife discovers the preacher doesn't always practice what he preaches. She expects him to be super-spiritual and he's not. Judy inspires me to grow spiritually but doesn't panic when I fail. She has one Jesus and doesn't expect me to be Him. She's not devastated when I'm not very joyous or pious at home. She very seldom quotes my sermon to me as a reminder

that I'm not practicing what I preached. While that may be true, it would be humiliating to hear.

9. Frequent encouragement—Thirty years ago my wife gave me a devotional Bible inscribed "To my husband, my friend, my lover, and my favorite preacher." She has repeatedly found ways to communicate respect and boost my ego over the years. Everyone needs a lot of encouragement. I'm no exception.

Few things have meant more to me over the years than Judy's discreet pat on my knee when I sit down beside her after I've preached a sermon. At that vulnerable, emotional moment, that simple gesture has so often reassured me that she thinks I've done well. Many times after a not-so-impressive sermon, on the way home from church she's assured me that the message was really pretty good even though she had to be tired of trying to boost up my fragile ego.

10. Total trust—Judy has a positive self-image, and I like the fact that she's been confident of her worth to me. She knows I could never find anyone to replace what she does for me, so very seldom does she get jealous or suspicious. I very seldom gave her a reason to be.

11. Unselfish attitude—(I know I said top ten reasons but I can't stop at ten.) We're all selfish at times. But Judy has been willing to serve and sacrifice herself more than almost anyone I know.

For forty years as the wife of the minister of Southeast Christian Church, she was content for me to be in the limelight while she assisted in the shadows. Over the years she served as the church pianist, nursery worker, Wednesday night cook (her least favorite job), women's ministry coordinator, women's choir director, tape ministry director, and book-store manager. She served on two major building commit-tees and various other church committees—and then politely smiled and graciously applauded when people praised me for the healthy growth of Southeast Christian Church. She very seldom complained about being taken for granted. That kind of unselfishness is rare . . . and special.

12. Classy demeanor—The first time I noticed Judy Thomas she was singing with a girls' trio at a conference in Cincinnati. She was poised and somewhat reserved. Opposites attract, and her classy appearance and unflappable conduct im-pressed me. Still does. She never got super-excited at my athletic achievements, nor did she whoop it up after one of my talks.

But she never embarrasses me and often coaches me in proper etiquette. She's helped me play it way over my head when I was squirming in sophisticated circles, and her tutoring has often saved me from embarrassment.

This already lengthy tribute would be longer if I took time to describe Judy as a good housekeeper, prayer warrior, efficient administrator, wise counselor, excellent mother, and adored grandmother. If no one else has read this far, I know that my wife will, because I'm important to her. So thanks, Judy. You're truly "the wind beneath my wings," and for fifty years God has honored us with "immeasurably more than what we asked or imagined."

Given the opportunity, I'd marry you again in a heartbeat!

Seems to me that tribute to her made up for some of my inattention and self-centeredness in those early years of marriage. But I still wish I could have a do-over.

5 ▶ I WOULD QUIT MENTALLY COMPARING AND COMPETING WITH OTHER PREACHERS AND OTHER CHURCHES

The reason we struggle with insecurity is because we compare our "behind the scenes" with everyone else's highlight reel.

—STEVEN FURTICK

There's an old poster that pictures Alaskan sled dogs from the perspective of the driver. The caption reads, "If you're not the lead dog the scenery never changes." Is that true for you? Do you have to be the lead dog, or you are dissatisfied with your position and status?

I have always been a competitive person. From the time I was a young boy I wanted to win; to be the fastest runner, score the most points, or be the first kid chosen. That's not all bad. Competition is healthy and normal. The late, great commentator Paul Harvey used to say, "It's each tree striving for a place in the sun that makes them all grow tall."

Understandably, I brought some of that competitive spirit into ministry. Early on I couldn't avoid comparing my church with others. My self-worth was in large part determined by attendance, offering, and baptism statistics. My mood during the week was impacted by the previous Sunday's stats.

A few years into my ministry, Southeast Christian Church was listed in a national religious magazine as the sixth fastest-growing church in America. That was a big ego boost . . . for about ten minutes. Then I began asking, "Who are those other five? Are they telling the truth? I wonder if we can get ahead of them and be number one next year."

On one occasion we hosted Max Lucado as a guest speaker. When I drove home after the Sunday morning worship service, my wife, who at the time was the overseer of our bookstore and tape ministry, was elated. She gleefully informed me, "We sold a record number of sermon tapes today. We sold 670 copies of Max Lucado's message."

I responded, "Judy, that's great!" Then I made a mistake. I asked, "What's the most of one of my sermons you've ever sold?"

There's always someone who has larger attendance, a nicer building, more accolades.

She said, "That sermon you preached on worry several months ago sold 250 tapes, but we sold 670 of Max's sermon this morning!"

I was a little depressed.

Now if she would have told me the Sunday I preached on worry that we sold a record number of tapes that morning, I would have been uplifted. But 250 compared to 670 isn't diddly-squat! So I was discouraged. And don't get me started on the time I compared my book sales to Max's . . .

Isn't that silly? Why do we insist on comparing ministries? Jesus asked Peter, "If I want [John] to remain alive until I return, what is that to you?" (John 21:22). If God chooses to bless another ministry in a different way than my ministry, why would I be jealous—if my heart is in the right place? Is it really about exalting Christ or exalting me? If it's really about advancing the kingdom of God and not advancing my own personal agenda, I should rejoice with every victory that's won.

Take it from someone who has been blessed to be in a church that grew steadily for a long time. Enough is never enough. If your self-esteem is dependent on you being the lead dog, you're always going to be dissatisfied and insecure because there's always someone who has a higher attendance, a nicer building, receives more accolades, speaks at a more significant conference, or sells more books. There's always a level above you, and if you insist on being the lead dog, you're going to wind up miserable and exhausted in ministry.

This is not to say that numbers are inconsequential. Someone counted 12 apostles, 120 in the upper room, 3,000 converted at Pentecost, and 5,000 men in the early church. Numbers matter because they represent people. The good shepherd counted the hundred sheep and discovered one was lost as a result of his concern for numbers. But numbers are valuable only in reference to our own experience, not in comparison with others.

That's why the Bible says, "When they measure themselves by themselves and compare themselves with themselves, they are not wise" (2 Corinthians 10:12). It's foolish to spend much time comparing your ministry with another because you are always comparing apples to oranges. Our talents are different. Our locations are different. Our lay leaders are different. Our communities are different. The effectiveness of other churches in our respective communities is different.

More importantly, God doesn't evaluate our effectiveness by attendance and offerings. Jesus said, "As he was scattering the seed, some fell along the path, and the birds came and ate it up. Some fell on rocky places, where it did not have much soil. It sprang up quickly, because the soil was shallow. But when the sun came up, the plants were scorched, and they withered because they had no root. Other seed fell among thorns, which grew up and choked the plants. Still other seed fell on good soil, where it produced a crop—a hundred, sixty or thirty times what was sown. Whoever has ears, let them hear" (Matthew 13:4–9). The difference isn't in the effectiveness of the sower, but in the receptivity of the soil.

It's also foolish to compare because the people who really matter don't care. My family doesn't measure my worth by the size of my church. My grandchildren don't care if I preach at a church of 18,000 or 18. They want to know if I'll get down on the floor and build a Lego set with them or play the Wii with them. So gradually I learned to be content regardless of the size of the church I served. I just wish I had a do-over so I could have felt that way at the beginning of my ministry.

ARE YOU CONTENT TO BLOOM
WHERE GOD HAS PLANTED YOU?

A good question for preachers to ask frequently is, "Am I a contented person?" The apostle Paul wrote, "I have learned to be content whatever the circumstances" (Philippians 4:11). Contentment doesn't come automatically; it's learned. And competitive preachers are usually slow to learn the lesson.

I visit with young preachers who are eager to climb the ecclesiastical ladder. They want to preach in an historic pulpit or a large church. They are so consumed with gaining a name for themselves they fail to enjoy the moment and bloom where they are planted. They are always restless, discontented with where they are at the present. They battle jealousy toward preachers whose ministries are going well. They are supersensitive to the latest brotherhood gossip about which church may be open soon. They ask friends to submit their name to pulpit committees of larger churches.

WHEN SHOULD A PREACHER LEAVE?

This raises an obvious question: when should a preacher consider going to another church? The apostle Paul moved from church to church on his missionary journeys. He was eager to preach the gospel in territories that hadn't been reached. So it's not selfish or overly ambitious for preachers to want their lives to have the most impact possible.

God does call us to new ventures and new challenges. But how do you know when it's time to leave? Obviously a change of ministry should not be motivated by unwarranted comparisons that result in jealousy and discontentment. But if God doesn't call you with a dramatic vision or audible voice, how do you know His will? Here are ten signs that suggest it may be time to start turning some doorknobs.

*1. Worship attendance declines for three years
in a row with no reasonable explanation.*

Sometimes there are valid reasons that a church doesn't grow. You serve in a small, depressed community and almost all youth move away. The main industry closes and the population of your town declines by 20 percent. Or maybe the church experienced a nasty split and the healing process is painfully slow. Or you've started several new church plants that have reduced the numbers at the mother church.

We shouldn't panic if attendance levels off occasionally. Even the best churches and businesses experience plateaus on occasion. But if attendance declines three years straight with no reasonable explanation it may be time to look elsewhere.

*2. In a secret ballot, one-third of
the elders suggest it's time to move on.*

If there's disharmony or lack of support at the core you are on shaky ground and it becomes very difficult to lead effectively. If you're wondering if it's time to leave, why not broach the matter with the elders and ask them to indicate their opinion in a secret ballot? If you are fearful that even asking the question would be a catalyst for division or unjust criticism,

Sometimes the Lord stirs up our nest, urging us to move out.

you may already have your answer. It could be just one rogue elder is stirring up unrest and would be exposed by that exercise and that could pave the way to healing.

3. You have made serious mistakes
that severely limit your ability to lead.

My friend Ben Merold stated, "We're like ships in the harbor; we all collect barnacles." If you stay in one place very long you will make mistakes with people. There was only one perfect Shepherd. If you collect too many barnacles, they can sink you. Perhaps you've offended unforgiving people who won't let it rest. Or your mistakes are so numerous and well known that you've lost influence with enough people that credibility can't be reestablished.

4. There is a prolonged inner feeling
of dissatisfaction where you are.

For some reason you just can't get your heart into your ministry anymore. You've lost your focus and your passion. Deuteronomy 32:11 teaches that an eagle "stirs up its nest" when it's time for a baby eagle to get out of the nest and fly on its own. Sometimes the Lord stirs up our nest, urging us to move out.

There are some cases where we get too comfortable and we know we're spiritually stagnant. We're restless because it's too easy and deep down we know we need a challenge. We don't want to spend the rest of our lives just coasting. A sense of prolonged internal unrest may be God prodding you to get out of the nest and fly.

*5. The salary from the church
cannot sustain you, or it insults you.*

We have no right to accept a church at an agreed-upon salary and then complain that it's insufficient. The Bible tells us to be content with our pay and trust the Lord to provide. But over a period of time an increase in salary is an indicator of appreciation and needs to be factored into our decision.

For the most part, preachers are paid better today than twenty or thirty years ago. But there are exceptions. And your needs change over time. If you have several children reaching college age or special needs children or elderly parents requiring care, maybe the current salary can't sustain you.

While salary is not the primary motivation for preaching, it is a factor to be considered. You have a responsibility to provide for your family, and salary is often a tangible indication of appreciation. Maybe an increase was promised that never materialized. Maybe your salary is significantly reduced because of shrinking offerings or it's been a decade since you had a raise. That may be a sign it's time to consider moving.

*6. A door is opening elsewhere that
challenges you and seems to be God's leading.*

The opportunity presented isn't one you've manipulated behind the scenes. You've not hammered doors down or pressured people into submitting your name as a candidate. But a door is spontaneously opening up and you identify with the apostle Paul's Macedonian call, "Come over . . . and help us" (Acts 16:9).

7. You are genuinely convinced your present ministry will do better in the long run if you leave at this time.

One of the reasons I left Southeast Christian when I did was because I sensed if I stayed much longer the church would lose the opportunity for Dave Stone and Kyle Idleman to lead them. They were both younger, more energetic, and very capable and eager to lead. It would have been unfair to ask them to wait any longer. I concluded the church would do better in the long term if I stepped aside.

8. It would be in the best interest of your family to leave now.

Perhaps the present ministry is too toxic an environment for your family. Your wife and children are your primary flock and they need protection. Another consideration is that there are seasons in the life of children more conducive to moving, before they begin school—sixth grade or ninth grade, for example. There are seasons in the life of your parents when they need you. One minister I know moved from Arizona to Kentucky because both his elderly parents were ill and they had no support. He felt obligated to care for his parents who were unable to move to Phoenix. You have a right to consider your family when you entertain the idea of moving on.

9. Close friends support the idea that you should entertain the idea of leaving.

Most friends don't initially tell you the whole truth. "No! Definitely not! Don't even think of leaving!" they insist. But after they think about it and pray about it, good friends who have their finger on the pulse of the congregation may admit, "You know, for your sake it may be best. We would be really disappointed if you left but you've got to do what's right." Their honest counsel is significant.

10. There is a sustained, undeniable
guidance by the Holy Spirit to a new ministry.

This is not a flash-in-the-pan feeling that can be attributed to hurt feelings or temporary discouragement, but a prolonged inner prodding that doesn't go away. You've consistently prayed and sought God's guidance and sense in your heart of hearts it's time to go.

That's when we trust that God's promise in Proverbs 3:5–6 will hold true: "Trust in the Lord with all your heart and lean not on your own understanding; in all your ways submit to him, and he will make your paths straight."

DON'T RESIGN IN ANGER

Whatever you do, don't resign in a huff. There will be meetings that anger you. There will be Sunday services that disappoint you. I see guys who, in hurt and frustration, resign in a tizzy with no place to go. They think, "The Lord will provide."

Good decisions are hardly ever made in haste.

I admire their faith, but I wouldn't recommend that. "Do you see someone who speaks in haste? There is more hope for a fool than for them . . . An angry person stirs up conflict, and a hot-tempered person commits many sins. Pride brings a person low, but the lowly in spirit gain honor" (Proverbs 29:20, 22–23).

God seldom is pleased when we jump off the pinnacle of the

temple and ask Him to catch us. Sure, your pride is wounded, but humble yourself for a little while longer and make a deliberate, wise decision. Good decisions are hardly ever made in haste.

It's easier to get a job when you have a job. You are more likely to find another church if you're still employed in one. If things are going poorly your leaders are more likely to give you a good recommendation if you're still on their payroll.

Instead of resigning in haste, have a heart-to-heart, transparent discussion with a trusted member of your church board. Chances are that leader will probably help you get a better perspective. An additional week or two spent in prayer and meditation will help you see the situation from God's vantage point. Don't resign in haste.

TAKE THE HIGH ROAD

When you decide it's time to leave, take the high road. Don't write a blistering resignation letter. Don't dump all your frustration in the final sermon. You'll never regret being gracious, forgiving, and gentle. Someone said, "If you can't be tactful, at least be vague." Be tactful and kind. Truth has a way of surfacing in time. If you don't defend yourself, others will. More importantly God will. He opposes the proud but He gives grace to the humble.

Before you resign in search of greener pastures, read Ecclesiastes 4:8. "There was a man all alone; he had neither son nor brothers. There was no end to his toil, yet his eyes were not content with his wealth. 'For whom am I toiling,' he asked, 'and why am I depriving myself of enjoyment?' This too is meaningless."

Maybe we ought to ask ourselves some basic questions: "Who am I trying to impress?" "Why am I so discontented where I am?"

"Is it because I'm trying to impress people?" "Am I still competing and comparing myself with others?" "Is my ego wounded because I'm not the lead dog?"

Someone said, "If you worry too much about what other people thought about you, you'd probably be disappointed to discover how seldom they did!" Perhaps it's time for me to take a major step of maturity and accept the fact that it's not all about me—it's about serving God and shepherding His people and learning to be content with where I am instead of making myself miserable with unrealistic comparisons.

My senior year in high school one of my goals was to be the leading scorer in Crawford County, Pennsylvania. (People look at my 5'9" frame today and have a hard time believing I ever played basketball. But I tell them I was 6'5" in high school. The church has a way of beating you down over the years.)

I was fortunate to play on a very good high school basketball team, and I was hopeful of being the leading scorer not just on our team but in the entire county. That was a big deal because the top ten scorers were listed every week in the Meadville, Pennsylvania, *Tribune*—and you don't get any bigger than the Meadville *Tribune*.

Every week my name was listed among the top three leading scorers. But one of the other names consistently near the top was a teammate of mine, Jim Komara. We were blowing teams away by huge margins and both of us scored similar totals. I confess that there were times when we were up by twenty points and Jim would shoot, I hoped it wouldn't go in. It was all about me!

However, at the end of the year our team was in the state tournament. The competition was stiffer and the games were close. Since it was single elimination, winning was paramount. In those crucial games, every time Jim Komara shot I desperately wanted him to make it. The good of the team became more important than my personal goals.

SEEING MINISTRY FROM GOD'S PERSPECTIVE

I can't point to an exact day or a specific experience when I concluded the good of the kingdom of God mattered more than my ego. But I did get to the point when I quit comparing. Slowly I became less competitive and more comfortable with the challenge to make the most of the opportunity I was given, regardless of what was happening elsewhere.

I never lost the zeal for evangelism or the desire to see the church grow, but I learned to be content regardless of fluctuating and unpredictable numbers. I could sincerely rejoice with others who were experiencing spiritual victories. I just wish it hadn't taken so long for me to get to that point.

John the Baptist's numbers went down the second year. Way down. But instead of being jealous of Jesus, John said, "He must increase and I must decrease." John knew it wasn't about him—it was about Jesus. Jesus praised John's team spirit by stating, "No greater man born to woman than John the Baptist."

6 ▶ I'D BE MORE GENEROUS TO INDIVIDUALS BOTH INSIDE AND OUTSIDE THE CHURCH

Remember, man does not live on bread alone.
Sometimes he needs a little buttering up.

—JOHN C. MAXWELL

Since my parents were actively involved in a church, I was trained to tithe to the church from childhood. My first paying job was hoeing weeds in a nursery when I was fourteen years old. Forty hours a week hacking at knee-high crabgrass and thistles is a tough assignment. My first paycheck amounted to $82, and I thought I was rich. I remember putting ten dollars in the offering plate on Sunday morning and thinking I'd been generous.

I've given at least a tithe to the church from that day on. It's been easier for me than most since I started living on 90 percent from the start. Over my forty-year ministry at Southeast Christian, our church went through six different building programs. That meant six fundraisers—what one of my friends teasingly called "annual shakedowns." With each campaign I felt the need to "be the example and not the exception," so I would make a three-year commitment, over and above my regular giving.

Like most people, I discovered when the three-year commitment was over, God had abundantly provided and it was easy to continue to give at a higher level. I've certainly not reached the giving level of a preacher friend who gives away 50 percent of his income, but I am making progress. The Bible instructs us to give in proportion to how we've been blessed and by that standard I'm probably way behind in what I should give. But in my mind I've been fairly generous with the church.

BEING A GENEROUS PERSON ALWAYS

But sometimes, under the guise of being a good steward of the rest, I would be tightfisted when I should have been liberal. I wish I had been more generous with parachurch organizations, needy persons, and those who served me outside the church. I know now I could have enhanced my witness to waiters and waitresses, bellboys at hotels, cab drivers, golf club attendants, mail carriers, paper deliverers, garbage collectors, and others who served, if I had been more generous with tips. I also wish I had given more generously to church members who were raising funds for mission trips or service organizations.

I wish I had reached out more to staff members and other preachers struggling with financial stress. God's Word says, "Freely you have received; freely give" (Matthew 10:8). For many years I was satisfied giving freely to the church and used that as an excuse to be overly frugal in other areas.

Wayne Smith was the very popular minister of the Southland Christian Church in Lexington, Kentucky, for over forty years. He was well known for his compassion and generosity. Several evenings each week he would stop at the local Kentucky Fried Chicken restaurant just before closing time, pick up the extra chicken that they were going to throw away, and deliver it to needy families before he went home.

Several times when I spoke at a rally around Lexington Wayne would come up afterward, and hand me a personal check as a supplement to the honorarium, because "You deserve more than they're giving you." He contributed generously to one of our fundraising campaigns—at a time when his own church was also in a building program. When my wife and I celebrated our fiftieth wedding anniversary, Wayne sent me twenty-five two-dollar bills!

I'd often brag about how generous Wayne Smith was. But for some reason it took too long to register in my mind that I should emulate that same spirit in my own life. A magnanimous spirit opens doors to witnessing to the lost and enhances credibility with believers. Jesus said, "I tell you, use worldly wealth to gain friends for yourselves, so that when it is gone, you will be welcomed into eternal dwellings" (Luke 16:9).

Howard Brammer is another preacher who excels in giving. Howard ministered to the Trader's Point Christian Church in Indianapolis, Indiana, for several decades. He recently related that he and a group of other board members of a parachurch organization went out to eat after their annual meeting. Following the meal, the chairman, a blustery preacher, said to their waiter, "Jeremy, we're a bunch of preachers here. We appreciate you serving us tonight and want to ask you if there's anything we can pray for you before we leave."

The waiter responded, "Well, as a matter of fact, there is. My wife has recently had some fairly serious health problems and has lost her job. As a result we're $487 behind on our gas and electric bill. If we don't pay it by the end of this week, our electricity is going to be turned off. Would you pray that God would somehow supply that need?"

The preacher led in a moving prayer and the waiter genuinely thanked them all. When the waiter left the chairman said, "Guys, let's be a real blessing to Jeremy. He needs help. I'm going to leave $20." The next guy said, "I'll give $10," the third put down $20, and finally it got to Howard Brammer and he counted the stack of bills and they had over $150 to leave as a tip. Howard said, "I'll tell you what guys, let's really bless this guy. I'll make up the difference and let's make it $487."

"Oh, no, Howard! You don't have to do that by yourself!" the others quickly blurted out. "I'll give $20 more." "I'll do the same." "I'll give $30 more." Howard said by the time it got around to him he counted it and he didn't have to give a dime! Not really. But his generous spirit was contagious. That day they left the waiter a $487 tip!

Howard said he often wondered how that waiter reacted when he picked up his tip. A year later he was back in the area and went to that same restaurant, hoping to see Jeremy. He was disappointed that he wasn't serving that night, but after the meal Howard asked his waitress, "Say, could you tell me, what's the biggest tip any server in this restaurant has ever received?"

She said, "You wouldn't believe it. A bunch of preachers were in here last year and they prayed with a waiter and then left him a

$487 tip." Then she added, "Would you pray for me?"

I guarantee you that today when the employees in that restaurant think about Christian preachers they think of them in a more positive light than a year ago. That's using worldly wealth to make friends for ourselves! It's also softening hearts to receive the seed of the gospel. I could have been a much better ambassador to the community if I had done that kind of thing more often.

BEING GENEROUS WITH ENCOURAGEMENT

I wish I had been more generous with encouragement too. While we appreciate receiving encouragement ourselves, for some reason most preachers aren't very good at encouraging others—especially other preachers. We are almost "standoffish" in our relationship with other ministers in our area or within the circle of our own brotherhood.

I once taught for a week in the Master of Ministry program at Kentucky Christian University. Preachers already on the field came back to the campus for a five-day seminar several times each year. In my class I required each preacher to bring a tape of a sermon they had preached in the previous year. Periodically during the class I'd select a tape at random and play a five-minute segment for the class to hear and evaluate.

That was usually a very uncomfortable five minutes for the preacher whose tape was selected. Most of us are self-conscious about our preaching and we dread evaluations—especially from our peers. Most of the guys were aware of those concerns and were tender and positive in their comments.

One afternoon I selected the tape of a youth minister who

was still in his twenties. When he heard his voice he immediately groaned in discomfort. Although he wasn't a very polished speaker, as we listened it was obvious that he had some very basic communication gifts and a high likeability factor that showed a lot of promise.

When I finished playing the sermon, the youth minister immediately apologized. "I'm not a preacher," he insisted. "I didn't have any formal homiletics courses. I didn't have much time to prepare. I know it's terrible." On and on he went with self-deprecation, trying to get ahead of the hurtful criticisms that he anticipated coming his way.

I asked him to be quiet and listen. There were several positive comments and a few tactful suggestions for improvement. Then I said to him, "You have no need to apologize. You have some very good communication skills. In fact your message was quite good. In my opinion you are really gifted and I think you ought to consider becoming a preacher in the near future."

Fifteen years later I received a moving thank-you letter from that guy. He said, "I want you to know your comments that day altered the course of my future. I had not considered the preaching ministry because I felt inadequate. But I was so encouraged that day in class that a few months later I accepted the call to a small church. Once I started preaching I loved it and the congregation responded well. I am now five years into a second ministry with a larger church that has a lot of promise, and my wife and I are extremely happy doing what we're doing. I just want to thank you for encouraging me that day in class. I love preaching! And those positive words from you catapulted me into ministry today. Thanks."

After receiving that note I wondered how many more young, uncertain ministers I could have encouraged if I'd been alert to the opportunity. I'd helped that young man because he was a student in a class I was teaching. But I could have repeated that experience many times over if I had been on the lookout for guys who needed it. And there are many.

I'm trying to make up for my deficiency in this area in my retirement. I'm conducting monthly mentoring retreats for preachers and trying to be an encourager to young preachers the way Barnabas encouraged Paul in the New Testament. Preachers get their share of criticism and often experience insecurity, so a little boost from an older minister sometimes means a lot.

Preachers, you could be a big boost to a minister in your area if you'd just send a brief email, "Hey, I got on your website this past week and listened to your sermon last Sunday. That really ministered to me and fed me. Thanks!" That would take just a little time and effort but would be extremely meaningful.

Those notes you take two minutes to write may be pasted on someone's refrigerator for months.

How about gathering three or four ministers in your area and meeting for breakfast once a month? After sharing mutual experiences and laughing about common goof-ups, pray for each other and encourage one another, "and all the more as you see the day approaching."

Text an associate minister on your staff and say, "That new program went really well. Thanks for all your effort. You are invaluable to our church." You'll be amazed at how meaningful just a little extra attention from you can be. Those notes you take two minutes to write may soon be pasted on someone's refrigerator for months.

I once heard Dr. David Jeremiah relate a story during a radio sermon about a couple in his church who struggled with their daughter through the terrible twos. It seemed like they were on their daughter's case all the time. She was cute but strong willed and not easy to handle.

Still struggling with her a year later, the father decided he'd try a new approach. He took his daughter out to eat by himself for her fourth birthday. He intentionally used the occasion to praise her for all her good attributes. "Honey, we want you to know that your mother and I love you very much. We think you are so special, and we are really glad you are our daughter. We love your sense of humor and the way you think for yourself. You are very gifted, and we know God is going to use you in a wonderful way. We're eager to see what you're going to become. We are really proud of you!"

Then that father stopped and reached to pick up his napkin from the table. His four-year-old daughter reached out and grabbed the back of his hand and pleaded, "More, Daddy. More!" Most of us get plenty of criticism and suggestions about how to do ministry. We need someone in our lives who will encourage us and boost us up. We can always use more of that.

THE MOST GENEROUS MAN IN THE WORLD

A few years ago I served on a parachurch board with the late Paul Meyer, who had the reputation of being one of the most generous men in the world. He began at age sixteen, collecting debits for an insurance company, and wound up making millions through selling insurance and then developing training programs. At the time I met him he was in his eighties and was giving away over 90 percent of what he made.

I sat at a table with Paul Meyer and his lawyer/accountant. His lawyer told me it was his job to make sure Paul didn't give away money faster than he made it—and that was a challenge at times. He told me that Paul had put over four hundred kids through college and had underwritten a number of worthy Christian causes.

He then related how the previous summer the two of them had taken an automobile trip of several hundred miles. During that two-day journey Paul Meyer offered to give ten teenagers he met along the way a full scholarship to college if they'd just call him.

Only one teenage girl believed him and took him up on the offer. She was working on highway construction, wearing a protective helmet, and holding up a stop sign. While they waited for traffic to pass, Paul Meyer rolled down his car window and called her over. "Young lady, why are you working on construction?" he asked.

"I'm trying to get enough money to go to college," she explained. "I have a dream of being a nurse someday, but my folks can't afford to send me to college."

Paul handed her his business card and told her, "Young lady, I'm in the business of making dreams come true. Call this number and I'll pay your way through college." He made nine other offers like that on that one trip. None of the others ever called. However, the next week that girl who had been working on construction called and said to the accountant, "Last week some little old man said he would pay my way through college if I called this number— could that be true?"

He said, "Yes, ma'am, it's true." Her way was paid through college and today she is a nurse in a Midwestern hospital. As the accountant shared that story I looked over at Paul Meyer, and he was beaming as he fought back tears of joy. I thought about that familiar Scripture, "It is more blessed to give than to receive" (Acts 20:35).

I don't have the resources of a Paul Meyer, but if I could turn back the clock I'd be a lot more generous with people both inside and outside the church. I know I could have softened many hearts and could have multiplied God's blessing on my life.

7 ▶ I WOULD NEVER AGAIN ATTEMPT TO COVER OVER A STAFF MORAL FAILURE

So if you find yourself in a difficult spot, remember:
you are there by God's appointment, in His
keeping, under His training, and for His time.
And all evidence to the contrary, there's no better
place to be.

—ROBERT J. MORGAN

Years ago in my ministry I had one of those *How am I going to handle this?* moments.

There was a guy on our staff whom I'll call Mark. He was gifted, likeable, worked well with the team. Mark and I were pretty close.

And one day I learned that Mark was cheating on his wife and had been for some time. I was devastated, disappointed, angry, and fearful. I pounded my fist against the wall out of frustration. I felt betrayed. Betrayed—and duped. How could I be so naïve? I was apprehensive about how his infidelity would impact our church. I was uncertain about what my course of action should be.

Later that morning I called Mark and left a message: "We need to talk." He sensed his secret was out and didn't return the phone call. Later that day he and his mistress took off, intent on leaving their families and beginning a new life together.

WHAT TO TELL THE CONGREGATION

That distressing news came on a Friday morning. And Sunday was coming. What was I going to say to the congregation? I immediately called the chairman of our elders and informed him of the situation. He called an emergency elders' meeting on Saturday morning.

After much discussion the elders wisely concluded, "Bob, here's what we'd like for you to do. Begin the service tomorrow by announcing, 'We regret to inform you that Mark has been dismissed due to a family problem. We ask you to pray for him and his family that there might be reconciliation. If you feel you need additional information, the elders will be in the lobby and you can talk with them individually.'"

Some preachers complain about their lack of support from elders and lay leaders. But I've been blessed over the years to have wise, godly elders who have encouraged me and provided good counsel. This was one of those times when they were a huge help. If I had gone on my own instincts that Sunday morning, I may have given too little information and the congregation would have felt we were covering something over, or I would have given too much detail and the congregation would have concluded we were throwing the associate under the bus and not giving him any chance for restoration.

The elders' balanced counsel and transparency that day was appreciated by the church. Our congregation was brokenhearted to hear the tragic news. But the church remained united and we went on to continued harmony and growth. The apostle Paul wrote, "Do not entertain an accusation against an elder unless it is brought by two or three witnesses. But those elders who are sinning you are to reprove before everyone, so that the others may take warning" (1 Timothy 5:19–20).

Paul's counsel is that when a leader stumbles and falls, the church should not cover it over and pretend nothing serious has happened. Leadership requires a higher standard. A leader's failure is to be made public, with discretion, so that others realize that sin is serious and the church is to be distinctive from the world. It also provides the most likely scenario for the fallen leader to be restored.

Truth has a way of stifling gossip and uniting a church.

Two days after announcing the dismissal of the staff member, I received a phone call from a young woman who had not attended the worship service on Sunday. She said, "Bob, there is a terrible rumor going around . . ."

I said, "That's not a rumor. That's the truth. I'm very sorry." Sometimes the truth hurts. But the truth also heals . . . and sets you free. In two weeks there was nothing more to talk about. Truth has a way of stifling gossip and uniting a church. Had we attempted to sweep the unpleasant truth under the rug, people would have been lifting up the rug and searching for dirt months later. I was thankful for elders who led in handling a terrible disappointment biblically.

SAFEGUARDS TO PREVENT IMMORALITY

Following that difficult experience I established some safeguards against immorality based on guidelines I had read that Billy Graham established for himself and his team. Billy Graham had a guiding principle that he would not meet, travel, or eat with another woman alone. It came to be known as the Billy Graham rule and has been widely embraced by evangelicals over the past sixty years to prevent infidelity or even the "appearance of evil."

I set forth the following principles for our church staff:

1. Staff members are not to ride in a car alone with a member of the opposite sex (other than their spouse) except in cases of emergency.
2. Staff members are not to meet a member of the opposite sex for a meal unless at least one other person is present.
3. Staff members are not to counsel a member of the opposite sex for more than three times. There is always to be a person in the adjacent room and preferably a window in the door.
4. Staff members are not to go into the home of a member of the opposite sex when there is no one else in the house (or the person is quite elderly).

Recently an article appeared in a national publication suggesting the Billy Graham rule should be discarded because it hasn't been effective in curbing infidelity. The author quoted a recent survey of 1,050 evangelical pastors in 2005–2006, in which 30 percent said they had been in an ongoing affair or a onetime sexual encounter with a parishioner.

According to the author, "The rule (often accompanied with a 'danger' story about an affair) has framed relating with the opposite sex with fear. When the other gender is kept at a distance, there is less chance for mutual respect and trust to grow. Our fear and distancing diminish mutual respect and create the kind of environment where inappropriate relating is more likely to occur."[1]

A total abstainer never becomes an alcoholic. A person who refuses to be alone with a member of the opposite sex won't have an affair.

I disagree. It seems obvious to me that 30 percent of ministers committed adultery because they failed to implement the Billy Graham rule. Those cautionary guidelines just make common sense. A total abstainer never becomes an alcoholic. A person who refuses to be alone with a member of the opposite sex won't have an affair.

When I occasionally shared our staff guidelines with our congregation in a sermon, business leaders would ask me for a copy. Since infidelity in the workplace created a major problem they were considering establishing similar rules at their place of business.

While those guidelines are helpful and establish important parameters and expectations they are far from being a cure-all. If leaders lack character, they find a way to disregard the guidelines and get involved in prohibited relationships.

ANOTHER MORAL FAILURE!

A few years after the devastating incident described above, I learned that another staff member was guilty of "inappropriate relationships" within the church. My immediate reaction was, "Oh, no! Not again! Our church can't go through this a second time. This will hurt so many people."

I looked for an easy way out and made two mistakes. First, I overlooked the reality that whenever you initially hear of a problem, it is usually a lot worse than what you learn at first blush. It's human nature to minimize the horrid nature of sin. For example, if you hear $3,000 has been embezzled from the church treasury, it's probably a lot more than that. So when I heard that there had not been actual physical intimacy involved, I wanted to believe it. I learned later that was a lie.

The second mistake I made was that I decided not to take the situation to the elders but to handle it on my own. If I went to the elders there would be no containing it. They would probably respond too harshly and a public disclosure would follow. Surely there could be some way out without bringing so much pain to the congregation.

I informed the erring staffer that I was aware of the "inappropriate behavior," and I set a two-month deadline for finding employment elsewhere. Otherwise, I would have to inform the elders. I also urged repentance, and confession and reconciliation at home. I was assured these things were happening.

A few weeks later I received a phone call from a church in another state asking for a recommendation for this associate, who had applied for an opening on their staff. They were impressed with what they saw and wanted my opinion about whether this person might contribute to their ministry. I now regret that I told them nothing but positive things. They were all true, of course. This person was quite gifted and had done many good things at our church. I simply didn't mention the dark side. I basically covered for our church . . . and myself.

When that church hired our associate, I breathed a sigh of relief. We provided a decent send-off, said all the expected things, and life went on. A few years later, however, that same person had another affair, got divorced, and tore apart another family in that church. To this day I regret mishandling that situation, and I feel partly responsible for two broken homes and a wounded church.

I wish I could turn back the clock. I wish I wouldn't have been so naïve and believed a lie. I wish I had taken the situation directly to the elders. I wish I had been totally honest in my recommendation to the other church. I wish I had learned from the earlier experience that handling disappointments with biblical transparency is always the best procedure.

HINTS FOR DEALING WITH LEADERS WHO HAVE FALLEN

When there is unethical or immoral behavior on the part of a church staff member I believe local church leaders would do well to respond according to the following guidelines.

(1) *Tell the truth and trust the Lord to handle the consequences.* We are tempted to speculate about all the scenarios that could happen, and then choose the path that seems the safest way out. The appropriate response is to be obedient to God's Word. We should "trust in the Lord and lean not to our own understanding."

If the Bible says to confront or to rebuke the offender, or to share the information publicly, then let's do what God's Word requires and trust the Lord to handle the consequences.

(2) *Don't focus on restoration until there has been evidence of repentance.* Our first reaction is to forgive, embrace, and attempt to expedite the restoration to fellowship and even leadership. But John the Baptist urged the Pharisees to "produce fruit in keeping with repentance" (Matthew 3:8).

When King David was confronted with his sin with Bathsheba, he quickly produced fruit in keeping with repentance. The evidence of repentance includes an open admission of guilt, a contrite spirit, a transformation of behavior, an attempt at restitution, and a willingness to assist others in overcoming the same temptations.

(3) *Remember God's kingdom is bigger than just your local congregation.* The temptation is to protect your territory and disregard what may happen in another church. The mature leader keeps the big picture. God's kingdom in another state is just as important as it is in your community. That means we handle problems God's way and don't try to secretly smuggle a flagrant offender into someone else's camp.

(4) *Be tactful but courageous when informing a search committee from another church about the negatives of a candidate.* If you are aware of serious character flaws or sinful patterns in the life of a staff person being considered, it's probably not wise to put your concerns in writing but do find a way to communicate them verbally. You are less likely to encounter legal complications while at the same time fulfilling your responsibility to be honest about potential problems.

(5) *See your church as more resilient than you imagine, and remember that sticky problems can stimulate maturity.* Shepherds tend to be overly protective of their flock. We want to shelter new believers from any disappointment and disillusionment. We can be so overly protective that they miss opportunities to mature in their faith. Even new Christians need to learn that human leaders have feet of clay. And better they hear it from you early on than from an outsider later. There is no minister who merits total allegiance. Only Jesus is worthy of our complete trust.

(6) *Expect the majority of the congregation to react as you do.* There's an old saying, "The mood of the leader is the mood of the team." If the church sees you are hurt but still able to move forward they will likely respond in much the same way. If they sense you are secretive or disingenuous they will lose confidence and wonder if it's all a sham. If they sense you are transparent and genuine, you will gain credibility.

Of course not everyone will follow your lead. Moses had critics who refused to follow him even though God parted the Red Sea under his leadership. So don't be shocked if some are suspicious or rebellious, but for the most part the congregation's reaction will mirror that of the minister.

"Blessed is the one who perseveres under trial because, having stood the test, that person will receive the crown of life that the Lord has promised to those who love him" (James 1:12).

PART 2

*What I Would
Do the Same*

8 ▶ I WOULD MAINTAIN PREPARATION FOR EXPOSITORY PREACHING AS A PRIORITY IN MY DAILY SCHEDULE

A prepared heart will make a prepared sermon.

—E. M. BOUNDS

After reading the first seven chapters of this book you probably believe I never did anything right in ministry. Admittedly, there were some serious mistakes. There were other things I wish I could have done differently. I wish I had started a junior high preachers' club to encourage young men to consider ministry. I wish I had kept a daily journal documenting how God was at work every day. I wish I had done a better job at taking time to celebrate victories instead of just hurriedly moving on to the next goal.

But in this second half I want to share some practices that I would repeat if given another chance. I did a few things right! I hope as I share some of them they will be helpful to you regardless of whether your leadership role is in the church or the marketplace. In 1 Corinthians 11:1, Paul said, "Follow my example, as I follow the example of Christ." I'm going to mention several things I would do much the same way if I had a do-over. These practices, I believe, are worth following. The first is that I would maintain preparation for expository preaching as a priority in my daily schedule.

MY FIRST FULL-TIME MINISTRY—A PREACHER'S DREAM

When I was a senior in Bible college, I accepted a weekend ministry at the Monterey Christian Church, which is located about thirty miles east of Cincinnati, Ohio. Monterey had been a weekend church for over a hundred years. There were some wonderful Christian people in that congregation, and I'm indebted to them for encouraging me as a young preacher.

Just before graduation I asked the Monterey elders, "Would you consider hiring me full-time? I don't want to be a bi-vocational minister and would like to stay here if possible." The church had been paying me $50 to drive out to preach on Sunday morning and Sunday night and to do an occasional funeral or wedding.

Following my request, the three elders held a two-hour meeting in which they finally made a decision to pay me $70 a week if I'd come full-time. I guess they figured I'd be worth $20 those other six days! That offer was contingent upon my agreeing to stay at least one year. I consented and it turned out to be a decision that would shape my ministry for the next four decades.

My first day on the field was just one week after my wife and I got married. At 7:15 on Monday morning Judy left for her job in Cincinnati and I was left sitting at the breakfast table. I remember thinking, "How am I going to spend my time? Should I go into town and strike up a conversation with people at the drugstore? Should I try to find some guys to play golf? Should I turn on the television and see what's on?"

Knowing my own nature and how easy it was to fall into bad study habits in school, I thought, "I may be establishing a pattern that will stay with me a long time." We lived in a little four-room house that had a small room we called "the study." In it was an old wooden desk, a metal chair we'd "borrowed" from church, and the few books I owned.

I determined, "If I'm not in that study by 8 a.m., I'm late." So at eight on that first Monday morning I started writing on my sermon for Sunday. When I was a student in Bible college, I could get up a sermon in four or five hours, maybe three hours if the chapel speaker was really good that week! Just a simple outline and a few illustrations to explain the Scripture, and I was ready. Now I had four hours to study every morning—alone.

Since the church had never had a minister on the field there was no office at the church building. No retirees were accustomed to stopping by to say hello to the preacher. And there were very few phone calls to interrupt me. I was left alone. It was a dream church for a preacher who is somewhat of an introvert. So by noon on Wednesday that first week, I had my sermon finished. I wondered, "What shall I do now?" I decided to write out the introduction. Then read another commentary or write out the conclusion. Before long I was writing and editing a sermon manuscript every week.

I also developed the custom of reading my sermon aloud at

least five times before preaching it. Though tedious, preaching the sermon out loud helped me avoid stumbling over words, not to become too tied to my notes, to stay within a time limit,

Time to be alone with God and His Word doesn't come easily for preachers.

and to develop a rhythm to my delivery. Within a few months I could tell I was getting better at preaching.

A LIFELONG DISCIPLINE

That discipline of spending twenty hours a week studying for a sermon stayed with me for the next four decades. When I accepted the call to Southeast Christian Church a year later, the environment was totally different. The church building was buzzing with activity every day. The phone rang frequently. People stopped by. So, I asked the secretary to hold all calls until noon unless it was an emergency. I asked the congregation to respect my study time in the morning—and most did. Later when we added staff members, they were asked to respect the same discipline.

James Earl Massey has said that he promised his new church, "If you give me time to be alone with my Bible and my God, I promise, you will not go home hungry or embarrassed." However, that time to be alone with God and His Word doesn't come easily for preachers. The longer you preach at one place the more difficult it is to give your attention to the Word of God and prayer.

In order for a minister to consistently find time to study he needs to be convinced of at least five truths.

(1) *The best thing you can do for your congregation is to feed them the meat and milk of God's Word each Sunday.* John MacArthur once told his Los Angeles church, "If I say yes to meeting with one person on Thursday morning I'm saying no to seven thousand on Sunday morning."

There's a time to meet with people—after all, the minister is to shepherd the flock. But meeting or counseling with members of the congregation shouldn't take precedence over study time. A practical slogan I was taught in Bible college was, "Study God's Word in the morning and God's people in the afternoon."

If you were going to start a new restaurant, what would you give attention to first? Not the print on the menu or the carpet in the dining hall or the ads in the newspaper. You would first give attention to the food. We've all seen restaurants that are holes in the wall, but jammed with people because the food is great. The best thing you can do for the health of your church week by week is to see that they are well fed.

(2) *Content matters more than delivery, and solid content takes study time.* A professional golfer once teased me, saying, "Bob, there are only two things wrong with your golf game: distance and direction." At first I was encouraged until I realized that's all there is! If you hit the ball straight and long, you will shoot par.

If you don't know much about golf you are first impressed with distance. You might conclude if someone hits the ball a long way they are a good golfer. But the more you observe golf, the more you realize that direction matters more than distance. That old guy who consistently hits it 180 yards straight down the middle is likely to beat the strapping teenager who hits it 300 yards behind a tree.

Assuming a preacher has a heart for God, there are only two essential elements to preaching: content and delivery. Those who don't know much about preaching are most impressed with delivery. "Wow! That guy can really preach! He could read the telephone directory and people would pay attention."

However, there is a big difference between a convention speaker and a pastoral preacher. A convention speaker can wow an audience with a dynamic delivery. But a pastor who gets up to feed the same people every week soon discovers that content matters much more than delivery. And substance, the bread and meat of the Word, takes time to develop. It doesn't just come off the top of your head on Saturday night.

A dynamic African American preacher shared that when he first started preaching he carefully prepared his introductory remarks—writing them out word for word. Then he said he just let the Holy Spirit lead him from there. That continued until one day a church member who had heard him preach for a few years asked, "Why is your part always better than the Holy Spirit's part?" He said it dawned on him that the Holy Spirit can work in preparation as well as presentation.

People who hear me preach for the first time will sometimes express surprise that I'm not a more dynamic speaker since I preached at a megachurch.

A few years ago I was a guest speaker at a Christian convention in Seoul, Korea. Several thousand worshipers were jammed into the meeting room and the worship was highly expressive. The men who led in prayer or made announcements were dynamic and forceful. I didn't speak Korean but I could just sense the excitement in the crowd's verbal response and affirmation of each speaker.

Since I'm a conversational-style preacher, that's not normally the kind of audience where I'm well received. Besides, I had to speak through an interpreter and I knew that was going to be tedious. I felt inadequate and uncomfortable. As I sat waiting for my time to preach, I handed a note to Don Waddell, my executive assistant. I wrote, "I think I'm in trouble!"—hoping to get some affirmation from him. Don took out his pen and wrote, "Just . . ." and I knew what he was going to say: "Just be yourself." But seconds later he handed me a note that read, "Just . . . pep it up a little!" That's not what I needed to hear! I could only be myself, and that's not super-dynamic.

Matt Proctor taught homiletics at Ozark Christian College for years. He told me, "Bob, we liked it when you came to speak in chapel because you motivated young guys to preach." I was encouraged by that, until he explained why. He said, "The guys had heard about your church and your preaching but after chapel they would come to my class and I'd ask, 'Well guys, what did you think?'"

Matt said the answers were usually quite similar. "We thought he'd be a lot taller." "His sermon was good but it was pretty simple." "He was a good speaker but not that dynamic." After a brief analysis they would conclude, "Hey, if he can do it we can do it too!" Matt said, "You really motivated guys to become preachers.'"

If the Lord used my preaching, it was due a lot more to the time spent in developing solid, logical, easy-to-follow content than in my natural speaking gifts. The apostle Paul wrote, "When I came to you, brothers, I did not come with eloquence or superior wisdom as I proclaimed to you the testimony about God. For I resolved to know nothing while I was with you except Jesus Christ and him crucified" (1 Corinthians 2:1–2).

(3) *You have to be convinced that study for preaching must take*

priority in scheduling. It's one thing to say preaching is a priority, but until it is a regular part of your weekly routine, study will inevitably be shoved aside as the pressure of the immediate takes precedence over the most important. It's my observation that more guys fail in ministry due to a lack of discipline of time than because of a lack of talent. I'm convinced my rigid discipline of studying the same time every week was a huge factor in my lengthy stay and the growth of Southeast Christian.

However, it's not enough just to be in the office at the same time every day because even there, all alone, there are distractions. This is especially true today with computers and cellphones. We intend to study but we first check emails or we are distracted by the ping of a text message and the flow of thought is interrupted.

Nicholas Carr said, "The Net seizes our attention only to scatter it."[1] Joanne Cantor in the book *Conquer Cyber-Overload* wrote, "When you're constantly being interrupted your brain is not operating at its full capacity."[2] When the phone buzzes we check to see who is contacting us and often respond on the spot, rationalizing, "This will just take a second." Social media is very distracting.

My suggestion to younger preachers is leave the cellphone with your secretary—or turn it off completely when you first walk into your office and don't check it until noon. When you sit down at your desk, go directly to sermon study, not to voice mail, not to letters, nor to administrative responsibilities. It's not just time that's needed—it's focused time.

(4) *We need to give the same effort the Sunday after Easter that we give on Easter Sunday.* It's easy for a team to get pumped up for the big game. But the great teams and the best players give maximum effort every time they take the field.

A reporter once asked Joe DiMaggio, New York Yankee legend, why he played so hard every day. While other baseball players sometimes coasted, DiMaggio never did. He responded, "Every time I walk through that tunnel and onto the field I imagine some young boy sitting up in the stands and this is the first time he's going to see me play. I want him to see me at my best."

Sometimes the way we tell the Lord we love Him is to walk into the study and begin writing a sermon when it's the last thing in the world we feel like doing at the moment.

The Sunday after Easter may be the first time—or the last time—someone will ever hear you preach. It may be a crucial time in someone's life and they desperately need to hear a word from the Lord. Every time we step into the pulpit those sitting in front of us deserve the best effort we can give. Sometimes the way we tell the Lord we love Him is to walk into the study and begin writing a sermon when it's the last thing in the world we feel like doing at the moment. Rick Atchley, the great preacher of The Hills Church in Fort Worth, Texas, suggests it's better to hit four singles in a row than to hit a home run and then strike out three times. I agree.

(5) *You have to be convinced that the most productive preaching is expository preaching.* The majority of the sermons I preached were expository sermons. I know there are many definitions of expository preaching. My goal was simple: teach a passage, apply it to people's lives. I preached through almost every book in the New Testament and most of the major characters in the Old Testament.

In Bible college I was taught to teach the Bible and illustrate the Bible. A light went on for me in preaching when that sequence changed to teach the Bible, apply the Bible, and then illustrate the application.

When I studied the passage of Scripture that was coming up next, my first question was, "Where does this passage apply? What need is met from this section of Scripture?" That need became the lens through which the entire passage was explained.

For example, if I came to Noah's flood in Genesis 6, the focus wasn't explaining the size of the ark and how many animals could fit inside. The focus was "Obeying God's Will When It Doesn't Make Sense." After dealing with a variety of examples of God's commands that go contrary to what we want to do I would say, "Today let's look at an example of a righteous man who was repeatedly commanded to take action that didn't seem to make any sense at all.

"Noah was commanded to build an ark when there was no water nearby—in fact he'd never seen it rain. Noah was commanded to preach repentance for years even though no one responded to the invitation. Noah was commanded to create stalls for animals in the boat even though he had not set one single trap. Noah was commanded to get into the boat because the flood was about to begin, but there was not a cloud in the sky." Then I'd seek to apply the story to times when God's commands don't make much sense today.

One of the reasons ministers shy away from preaching expository sermons is they go to church conferences and hear famous preachers relate how a series on "Recovering from Addictions" or "How to Have the Best Sex Life Ever" increased their attendance by 25 percent. They note how cutting-edge preachers do four-week series with catchy titles and impressive staging and backdrops and conclude, "Maybe we're boring people with all this Bible teaching. We need to get with it." So they plan an increasing number of short series on marriage, stewardship, and current events, and television themes.

I think that's a mistake. God can bless topical preaching. We've all witnessed that. Whether you take the horse to water or bring the water to the horse, it still gets a drink. But I think, in the long run, expository preaching is healthier than topical preaching—for everyone.

This is one case where a congregational survey may prove otherwise, especially with newer believers. Ask young believers if they prefer a series on the book of Ruth or a series on "Girls Gone Wild" and most would probably choose the latter. But I would encourage preachers to have more confidence in the power of the Bible and less concern about what's trendy.

Expository preaching gives preaching *balance*. It avoids pet themes and gives context to relevant topics.

Expository preaching *feeds the preacher*. There's a big difference between writing a topical sermon and searching for proof-texts to verify what we want to say and writing an expository sermon that begins with a text that determines its meaning and application. When the preacher is digging into the text and reading a variety of commentaries he is edified and he is preaching from the overflow.

Expository preaching *edifies the believer*. Our task is to feed the flock the milk, bread, and meat of the Word of God. In this era of a diminished emphasis on Sunday school and increased emphasis on relationships in small groups, it's vitally important that the weekend sermon teaches the congregation more Bible content.

Expository preaching *meets unfelt needs*. We hear a lot today about preaching to felt needs. But there are needs that we don't know about that only the Word of God can meet.

Expository preaching *meets the need of the seeker*. One of the biggest objections to expository preaching is that it bores the unbeliever. Some suggest the visitor will not connect with verse-by-verse teaching through the Bible. That has not been my experience. If we are creative in finding relevant application, the Word of God is also powerful in penetrating the needs of the seeker's heart.

In his book *Overhearing the Gospel*,[3] Fred Craddock points out seekers actually hear the gospel better if they think it's not directed at them. They're not on the defensive. For example, picture a couple having marital problems attending a wedding. The preacher speaks to the bride and groom about the qualities that make for a successful, lasting marriage. The troubled couple sitting in the congregation may receive the message better than if the minister were sitting across the counselor's desk speaking directly to them. Their defenses are down and they don't feel singled out.

The seeker or skeptic hearing a sermon that is focused on how the believer should respond to God is more likely to receive it well than if he/she is targeted.

That's why I encourage preachers to make 90 percent of their preaching expository—just going through a book of the Bible. I really believe the four-week series that is popular with many preachers today would be more effective if it came on the back end of an eight-week series through the book of Ephesians or a twelve-week series through the life of Moses than if it's just following up another four-week topical series from last month.

I like the way *The Message* paraphrases 2 Timothy 4:3–5: "You're going to find that there will be times when people will have no stomach for solid teaching, but will fill up on spiritual junk food—catchy opinions that tickle their fancy. They'll turn their backs on truth and chase mirages. But you—keep your eye on what you're doing; accept the hard times along with the good; keep the Message alive; do a thorough job as God's servant.'"

"WHAT HAPPENED TO THE SHEPHERDS?"

Shortly after I retired Judy and I visited a church the first Sunday in December. That morning the preacher announced, "Today we're beginning a Christmas series on 'The Perspectives of Christmas.' Our associate will preach today on 'The Perspective of the Shepherds.'"

The associate had just one line about the shepherds at the beginning of his sermon. He said, "The shepherds were abiding in the field at night when suddenly they looked up into the sky. And that's what I want to talk about today. I want you to think about the vastness of the universe God has created."

He went on for twenty-five minutes on the immensity of the universe. He quoted statistics from astronomers about how long it takes light to travel from the nearest star, how big Betelgeuse is. He showed a picture of earth—just a tiny dot from outer space. But he never came back to the shepherds.

When we left I thought, "I'm too critical of preaching. I'm not going to say anything to Judy about it. Maybe she got a lot out of it." We walked to the car. She shut the door, looked at me, and asked, "What happened to the shepherds?"

It's strange. I've been going to church for seventy-two years. I know the story of the shepherds like the back of my hand. Yet when I go to church at Christmas I still want to hear that old, old story about the shepherds. Get me inside their robes. They were sore afraid. How afraid is that? After the angels left did anyone volunteer to stay with the sheep? Did they have a hard time finding the stable? Was Mary reluctant to let these smelly shepherds hold the baby? Did they kiss Him on the forehead? The Bible says they returned "glorifying and praising God" . . . did anyone hear them in the middle of the night? Were they told to be quiet?

Just maybe you might say something fresh I never thought about. But even if you don't, there's something about that familiar account that feeds me. C. S. Lewis said we don't need to be taught new ideas so much as to be reminded of old truths. Jesus said, "Man doesn't live by bread alone but by every word that comes from the mouth of God" (Matthew 4:4).

9 ▶ I WOULD MAKE THE NECESSARY ADJUSTMENTS TO COPE WITH THE TAXING PRESSURES OF MINISTRY

Often it's not the mountain ahead that wears you out—it's the little pebble in your shoe.

—MUHAMMAD ALI

Peter Drucker, the well-known business consultant and analyst, influenced a number of leaders from a wide range of organizations across all sectors of society. He was hailed by *Business Week* as "the man who invented management." Drucker once said the three toughest leadership positions he could imagine were a hospital administrator, a university president, and a megachurch pastor. The reason those assignments were considered difficult was because the leader is required to wear so many different hats and to meet the demands of so many different people.

Having been the minister of both a large and a small church, I have concluded that all ministers have a challenging, stress-filled job because so much is expected of them: preacher, teacher, counselor, administrator, organizer, committee chairman, visionary, community influencer, bus driver, coach, youth sponsor, custodian, and senior citizens program director. The expectations are endless.

WHY THE MINISTRY IS STRESSFUL

Every minister feels the pressure every day. The preacher is *constantly onstage.* You are expected to be nice to people all the time. You are expected to live an exemplary life every day. I've had people say to me, "Preacher, I saw you at the basketball game the other evening. I had my binoculars on you during the timeout. I was watching to see how closely you were observing those girls in the dance team." Unbelievable!

A humorous teenage boy in our church would often ask me, "Preacher, are you on duty or off duty right now?" An experienced preacher knows he's never really off duty. He's being carefully observed all the time. Not just behind the pulpit but at the grocery store, his kid's ballgame, the golf course, or mowing his front yard. That can be exhausting and stressful.

The longer we're in ministry the more we understand *what we are doing is critically important.* We are impacting lives and families for eternity. We've all had people say, "I was considering suicide until you came to visit me in the hospital." "I was about to give up on the church when I heard your sermon." Or, "We were about to divorce when you counseled us and today we're so glad we're together." Or, "I would have never known the Lord, I would be going to hell if you hadn't taught me about the grace of God." That's wonderful! But it's also a lot of pressure to be involved in matters that impact people's lives for eternity.

The moral standards for a minister are higher than any other occupation. A CEO can get a divorce, a pilot can drink when he's off duty, an athlete can bet on a sport that's not his own, an accountant can lose his temper and curse, a teacher's children can get arrested for shoplifting—and those people retain their jobs. But any one of those activities could be grounds for dismissal from the pulpits of most churches.

> **Writing a sermon is like having a term paper due every week.**

There's the pressure of *dealing with tragic circumstances in people's lives.* I will never forget the phone call informing me that a young father had run over his beautiful three-year-old daughter with his truck. He was cutting down a tree in the front yard and needed to move the truck just a few feet and didn't know she was playing under the back wheel. What do you say to that couple? What do you say at the funeral?

I'll never forget going into the home of a middle-aged couple who had just been informed that their twenty-one-year-old son, an outstanding tennis player, had dropped dead of a previously undisclosed heart defect while he was exercising. Dozens of friends were at their house trying to comfort the distraught parents. I was escorted up to their bedroom where they were both sitting on the floor beside their bed, uncontrollably sobbing their hearts out. All I could do was sit down beside them and weep with them.

Then there is *the relentless pressure of getting up a sermon every week.* Only a preacher understands the stress of living under the awareness that Sunday is coming and we need to have something fresh and meaningful to say. It's like having a term paper due every week. And the clock starts ticking the minute you walk out of the pulpit on Sunday. We're often a different person on Friday than Monday because of the escalating stress we feel.

Wayne Smith, humorous, outspoken minister of the Southland Christian Church in Lexington, Kentucky, for many years, said he preached his heart out twice one Sunday morning and again on Sunday night. When he arrived home, exhausted, his wife was sitting in the family room and whispered, "Shhhh . . . Charles Stanley is on TV."

Wayne quipped, "You know what? When you've preached three times on Sunday, you don't want to come home and watch Charles Stanley on TV. You want to see Clint Eastwood kill somebody!" Only preachers know how funny—and realistic—that is.

Add *the pressure of a few critical people who are never pleased with anything* and the ministry is tough. It takes a rugged mentality to survive the Monday-morning quarterbacks in the church.

The apostle Paul listed all the hardships he had experienced over the years—stoned, shipwrecked, imprisoned. Then he wrote, "Besides everything else, I face daily the pressure of my concern for all the churches." Paul felt the pressure from the church that we all feel.

I'M JUST DRAINED!

Several years ago I received the following email from a young, very effective minister. "Bob, I am really struggling right now with an issue I've heard you speak about several times. I am feeling stretched way too thin in my ministry and I'm getting to the point where I'm not doing anything very well.

"I'm not struggling with any kind of sin or immorality. I'm dealing with feelings of inadequacy and depression. I'm just drained. And my personal walk with Christ seems nearly nonexistent.

"I need to refocus. As the church has grown I have become bogged down in administration and I'm horrible at administration. My gift is preaching and teaching. I feel that's where I need to focus and then secondly to begin investing in people's lives. Please pray that God will lead me in this transition."

That email expresses the frustration of a lot of preachers. It's not the criticism or ego that destroys most ministers. It's coping with the daily pressures and demands that leave us drained. No wonder we all have friends and former colleagues who have left the pastoral ministry for another line of work. The pressures are just too grinding.

HOW I DE-STRESSED

I'm occasionally asked by young ministers how I survived a high-profile, high-pressure ministry for forty years. Looking back, I can see a number of things the Lord brought into my life, some deliberate, others unintentional, that really helped me cope with stress.

(1) *I learned to take a day off.* I've already mentioned Dr. Matthew Sleeth, author of the thought-provoking book *24-6: a Prescription for a Healthier, Happier Life*, which emphasizes the importance of practicing the Sabbath principle. I decided early on that Saturday was my day off. My two sons were home from school on Saturday

and I could spend time with them. I determined to have my sermon finished by Friday, and Saturday was a relaxed day.

Years later, when we started a Saturday night church service because of crowded conditions it negatively altered my schedule. I scrambled to take Tuesdays off during the last decade of my ministry, but it was never quite the same. That's why I recommend to ministers that they move to a Saturday service only as a last resort. It puts additional pressure on young staff members and their families when leaders have to be in church early Saturday afternoon.

(2) *I developed a daily quiet time early in ministry.* The first few years my devotional time was sporadic. Then an intern said to me, "I'm doing a paper on prayer. I don't think most Christians pray much. Have you prayed today?" My answer was embarrassing. I stumbled around about praying on the way to work and praying before mealtime. But I knew what he was asking, "Did you have a quiet time today?" And the answer was no.

That convicted me, and I determined that was going to change right then. So every day, from that time on, the first thing I do in the morning is "go into my closet" and kneel and pray. I pray out loud because it helps me to concentrate and to finalize thoughts.

> **I recommend to ministers that they move to a Saturday service only as a last resort.**

When I read about Martin Luther and some of the saints of the past spending two hours a day in prayer, I'm embarrassed because my prayer time is not that lengthy nor intense. But I do take time to thank God for yesterday's experiences and answered prayers and then lay before Him the needs of that day. Then

I pray for my family and a list of missionaries and people in need.

Afterward I read one chapter from the Old Testament and one from the New Testament, underlining passages that are meaningful to me. Most of the time I conclude by reading a section of a Christian book. And that's it. But it's a meaningful fifteen or twenty minutes to me.

We charge our cellphones every night so they can function for the next day. But we pastors too often fail to recharge ourselves. Yet Jesus taught us to pray, "Give me this day my daily bread." Jesus often withdrew from the crowds to spend time alone with His heavenly Father. Obviously we need that too.

I once came in late to a preachers' luncheon. When served my meal, I briefly bowed my head, closed my eyes, and expressed thanks. When I started eating a blustery older preacher from the other end of the table barked, "Brother Russell. That was an awfully short prayer!" I said, "Roy, if you prayed more often, you wouldn't have to pray so long!"

My mother used to talk about "staying prayed up." A daily quiet time contributes to staying prayed up and lays the groundwork for "praying without ceasing."

(3) As I mentioned earlier, *I preached mostly expository sermons.* Some of my best times with the Lord came when studying to explain and apply challenging Scriptures that came up as a result of preaching through a book of the Bible. Expository preaching feeds and fortifies the preacher to cope with stress.

(4) *I had a hobby that had nothing to do with the church.* Preachers should be devoted to the church and love the church. But we don't need to be consumed by the church. It's healthy for church leaders to have interests outside the church so that if church work is

troublesome or stagnant we have something else to look forward to. It's been said we all need something to do, someone to love, and something to hope for. A hobby outside the church gives us something to look forward to. For years I really enjoyed playing softball. When I was younger our competitive church team got involved in tournaments, and one summer we played over eighty games! I performed a few weddings with my softball uniform under my suit so I could make it to the game on time. As I grew older I enjoyed playing golf and attending University of Louisville football and basketball games.

I have preacher friends who enjoy fishing, skiing, hiking, woodworking, and coaching Little League. My brother-in-law, who is a preacher, belongs to a bicycling club.

A preacher friend of mine in Louisville loves to referee basketball games. I don't understand why but he really looks forward to going home at the end of the day, putting on a striped shirt, driving thirty miles outside of town, and officiating an important high school basketball game where no one knows him. Fans sometimes criticize a call and even scream profanity at him but he just brushes it off and says, "I've been to elders' meetings; I've dealt with worse," and takes his $100 paycheck and drives home. For a few hours the church is not on his mind and he's able to start the next day refreshed.

(5) Another thing that helped me cope with pressure is that *I had close friends with whom I could vent.* I learned a lot of good things in Bible college. But one piece of advice I received was not good. I was told, "Don't have any close friends in the church." I know the motive behind that counsel—don't play favorites; others in the church will be resentful. Or you can get too close to some people and share information that they can use against you later.

But if Jesus had three disciples who were closer than others because He needed friendship, so do we. I was thankful that over the course of time I developed friends in the church who were totally trustworthy and with whom I could be myself. I tried to practice some discretion so most in the church didn't know who my closest friends were, but I could go to these individuals when under stress and unload. They would understand without judging me and would often give encouragement and practical advice.

I could say, "You wouldn't believe what this church member said to me—it really hurt me." They would say, "Don't worry about that guy. He has zero influence." I'd say, "Yeah, but he's just a jerk sometimes." And I would go home feeling so much better. I didn't have to worry about my friend ever repeating what I said. He knew me well enough to know I still loved the guy and wanted to minister to him even if he was a jerk sometimes. My friend understood and gave me a channel to vent frustration and go on.

(6) *It helped me to share the pulpit on occasion.* Every summer at the end of our brotherhood's annual convention, I exchanged pulpits with Wayne Smith, the minister from Lexington. That meant during the convention we didn't have to feel the pressure of writing a new sermon. We could preach one from the past year that we liked and both churches benefited.

I soon learned that it was helpful to me to have someone else on staff preach, and I could spend that week giving attention to administration and pastoral care and be out from under the pressure of another term paper due. That practice also helped develop other preachers such as Dave Stone, who became my successor, and reminded the congregation that we were focused on Christ and we were not a personality cult.

(7) *Missions trips really helped me to cope with stress, and reenergized me for ministry.* Some people absolutely love going on mission trips.

There's something healthy about being totally isolated from local ministry.

They eagerly anticipate them. I didn't. I dreaded them. I don't like eating food when I don't know what's in it or sleeping in beds when I don't know what's in it. Every trip I took, I counted the days until I was home.

But I liked what mission trips did for me. When I got back home I had a fresh perspective on my responsibilities. There's something healthy about being totally isolated from local ministry. There's something about meeting Christians in third world cultures who have so little but are so joyful that is convicting in a healthy way. There's something about taking risks and getting out of your comfort zone and having to trust God that deepens you spiritually in a way nothing else does.

So I have been to Cuba, the Dominican Republic, Kenya, Poland (twice), China, Korea, and India on mission trips. India was the most difficult and the most beneficial for me. I'm not sure I was as helpful to the Indian missionaries as I should have been, but they were very gracious to me.

While in central India, at a mission called Mid-India Christian Mission, I got sick early on in the trip, and my friend Jay Henry and his family were very helpful and understanding. After I recovered, I kept experiencing an increasing pain in the calf of my right leg.

We traveled a considerable distance to a preaching point three hours away from electricity. I came limping into the cafeteria for lunch, and a doctor on the trip said, "Let me look at that leg." His eyes lit up and he announced to the mission team, "Folks, we have a serious problem here. Bob's got deep vein thrombosis. He has a blood clot in his leg and we need to head back toward the mission immediately so we can find some blood thinner. This is a life-threatening problem."

I knew a little about blood clots and figured my chances were pretty good, but it was still sobering to know my life was endangered. Most of us wonder how we'll cope when something serious threatens us. I discovered God's Word is true: The Holy Spirit lifted me up and I was not at all fearful. In fact, I joked about it. Our church had just borrowed millions to finance a massive building project we were in. The banks had required a "key man life insurance policy" be taken out on me, worth half the loan.

I was worth more dead than alive! I told people I was a little afraid to walk across the street for fear that some elder would say, "Let's take a hit for Jesus!" In India when I learned I had phlebitis, I said to one of the mission team members, "If I die out here can't you just hear Dave Stone (associate minister) next Sunday? He'll say, 'Folks, we've got some bad news . . . and some good news! The bad news is our preacher died. The good news is we're close to being debt-free.'"

I begged the doctor accompanying us on the trip not to let me wind up in an Indian hospital. He assured me that wouldn't happen. But when my situation became too complex, we had no option. So while most of the mission team flew home, I stayed behind for a week in an Indian hospital until the blood clot had completely dissolved.

During that time, I never felt farther from home, but I also never felt closer to God. I knew that for me to have my most serious health problem halfway around the world was no coincidence. God was reminding me of His care and His presence to lift me up.

The Sunday I returned to the pulpit, I was so grateful to be back home and so filled with the Holy Spirit that many said that message was the most memorable sermon they ever heard me preach. The congregation and I rejoiced together that God had brought me through an uncertain time. That edifying experience would have never happened had I stayed in my comfort zone at home.

(8) *The most helpful practice that enabled me to last forty years in the same ministry was an annual summer break.* After almost twenty years at Southeast I asked the elders if I could take a sabbatical. I explained that I was drained. I needed a rest, but more importantly I needed to replenish my spiritual well. I was running on empty.

They asked, "How long would you like to be gone?" I said, "I'd like to be gone for four or five months." They balked at that idea. "We're in a building program and that's not practical or wise for you to be gone that long." After considerable discussion someone suggested, "Bob, you take three weeks of vacation every summer. Why don't you take an additional two weeks every year as a study-break? Go visit other churches, read, and study."

The elders were in agreement and for the final half of my ministry that's what I did. I took the entire month of July off and was gone five weekends in a row. Sometimes in May I felt like I was holding on by my fingertips and would think, "If I can make it for another month I'll be okay." Sometimes when I would leave for the summer break, I didn't care if I ever came back. But those five weeks every summer rejuvenated my spirits. Every time.

The first week I didn't do much of anything ministry-related. Our family would spend the time at a cabin in the Smoky Mountains and I would relax and rest. The second week I would visit a Christian bookstore in Knoxville and end up buying a couple hundred dollars' worth of books. Then I'd go back to the cabin and start reading and thinking about a possible sermon series.

The third week I'd start forming a sermon to preach when I returned and by the fourth week it was finished and I was eager to get back. By the time I came back after five weeks I couldn't wait to preach again and the congregation seemed eager to listen. That renewed spirit couldn't happen for me in just one week.

In fact most preachers don't really take a vacation anymore. They schedule eight to ten days away with their family but they take their laptop and their cellphone and they run the church from two hundred miles away—just like always. Nothing much has changed except they're cramming in an afternoon at the beach or the amusement park with their kids. There is very little release from their daily pressure. In some instances they return more exhausted than when they left. And they wonder why they have so little passion for their assignment.

Jesus' ministry lasted just three and a half years. Yet He spent the first five and a half weeks alone in the wilderness preparing for what He was going to do. We would be more effective if we would follow in His steps.

Oswald Chambers summed it up well: "If I am devoted to the cause of humanity only, I will soon be exhausted and come to the place where my love will falter; but if I love Jesus Christ personally and passionately, I can serve humanity though men treat me as a doormat."[1]

10 ▶ I WOULD AGAIN LAUGH A LOT AND INCORPORATE HUMOR IN MY PREACHING

Our sense of humor is a gift from God that should be controlled as well as cultivated. Clean, wholesome humor will relax tension and relieve difficult situations. Leaders can use it to displace tension with a sense of the normal.

—J. OSWALD SANDERS

When my son Rusty was in the second grade he was given a thought-provoking writing assignment. He was asked to fill in the following blank: "I like it when _____. " Rusty wrote, "I like it when my dad laughs." That brief essay absolutely thrilled me.

It's my nature to be quick to laugh. I think laughing out loud is one of the healthiest things a person can do. The Bible says, "A cheerful heart is good medicine" (Proverbs 17:22). The writer of Ecclesiastes wrote, "There is a time to laugh" (3:4).

In his book *The Humor of Christ*, D. Elton Trueblood, American

Quaker author and theologian, pointed out that Jesus excelled in first-century humor—exaggeration. People in the first century laughed at hyperbole and embellishment. Trueblood suggests Jesus' audience must have laughed out loud when Jesus talked about straining at a gnat and swallowing a camel or taking a speck out of someone's eye with a saw log jutting out of your own or a camel trying to squeeze through the eye of a needle.[1]

Jesus was a man of joy. Just hours before His anticipated arrest and suffering, He told His followers, "I have told you this so that my joy may be in you" (John 15:11). A healthy sense of humor is a tangible evidence of joy in us.

THE IMPORTANCE OF LAUGHTER IN CHURCH

Laughter is an invaluable virtue in ministry. It's needed to counter the many heartbreaking experiences in the life of a church. Children get sick and die. Marriages break up. People lose their jobs. Christian leaders stumble and fall. We need to be reminded frequently that the joy of the Lord is our strength. A sense of humor helps us avoid becoming jaded and melancholy. Henry Ward Beecher said, "A person without a sense of humor is like a wagon without springs jolted by every pebble in the road."

Robert Louis Stevenson once entered a note into his diary that read, "I have been to church today, and I am not depressed." That seemed unusual to him. It shouldn't have been. Church should be a place where people hear good news and sense a spirit of joy on the part of those who believe the gospel. One of the characteristics of a healthy, growing church is that members are quick to laugh. A church that is divided or dying usually is unresponsive to humor.

Laughter is contagious. A joyful spirit attracts others. Butch Dabney was one of the founding elders of our church. He was noted for his joyous spirit and uplifting humor. For years he served as a volunteer worship leader and choir director. When I arrived, four years after the church was founded, I discovered Butch's joyful spirit had just permeated the church. Southeast Christian Church was a place with contagious laughter.

Butch might say to an outstanding pianist, "That was great, why not use both hands this next time through?" Between songs Butch would ask the congregation, "Do you know why a hummingbird hums? It doesn't know the words! Now you've got the words in front of you so let's sing them like we mean them."

Butch aged gracefully and kept his sense of humor into his older years. Once I was teaching a Saturday morning men's Bible study on the subject of aging and dying. I asked, "Do you fear death more or less as you get older?" All the older guys insisted they feared death less. When I asked, "Why is that?" Butch chirped, "It's because you've got more friends in heaven than you've got on earth!"

At the church's fortieth anniversary celebration we asked Butch to share an overview of the first eldership with the congregation. He was past eighty at the time. When it was his time to speak, Butch shuffled into the pulpit with a twinkle in his eye and said, "There were five founding elders. Four are dead. And I don't feel very well myself," and he turned and sat back down. That was it! The congregation roared with laughter.

After a Sunday visit to Southeast Church one respected journalist for *The Christian Standard* wrote, "If I could sum up Southeast Christian Church in one word it would be the word 'joy.'" She went on to elaborate that it wasn't just laughter but a spirit of joy that

Humor is serious business with me.

seemed to permeate the whole church that made it so contagious.

An experienced sound technician once wrote a letter to me about our church's radio sermons. He wanted to know who did our "laugh track" because it was the cleanest and most authentic he had ever heard. I was delighted to inform him that it wasn't a laugh track at all, it was just . . . us.

THE USE OF HUMOR IN PREACHING

Ministers can teach their church to be joyful by an appropriate use of humor in preaching. Some preachers frown on anything lighthearted in the pulpit. But humor is serious business with me. I was intentional about trying to find something funny to include each week. Webb Garrison in *The Preacher and His Audience* argues that humor is a powerful, persuasive tool. "It is an affront to the God we serve to neglect the skillful use of humor in our preaching."[2]

Appropriate humor in preaching is indeed a powerful, persuasive tool. It commands attention. People who've been half-listening sit up and wonder what they missed if the congregation laughs out loud. They ask, "What did he say?"

It communicates joy. Regardless of what's happening in the world, the church is a place with good news. Laughter reminds us of our hope, and presents a contrasting environment with the world.

It enables participation. Unlike predominantly black congregations, most white churches are hesitant to say "amen" or affirm the preacher aloud. Laughing sometimes assures the preacher of the congregation's involvement with the message.

It provides comic relief. One pastor in California told of a nervous bride who could not say the words "till death do us part." She attempted it several times to no avail. The congregation started to laugh nervously. Finally the pastor said, "Well, would you settle for a couple of years?"

Humor breaks down barriers. Once during a series on difficult issues, I was scheduled to preach on "Women's Role in the Church." Knowing it was a difficult and controversial subject that had some uptight, I began the message by barely whispering, "I apologize. I've developed a bad case of laryngitis and am unable to speak. I'm going to ask our associate to share his views on this subject." It was both comic relief and served to break down cultural barriers.

It clarifies a point. Jerry Vines said, "The purpose of humor in the pulpit is not to get laughs but to drive home the point in an entertaining way."

It provides a change of pace. Dave Stone, current pastor of Southeast Christian, has a wonderful sense of humor. He explains, "Humor can be like a breath of fresh air to a person who has been underwater for a minute."

It softens hard hearts. Christian comedian Grady Nutt billed himself as "The Prime Minister of Humor." He was a master at using humor to soften hearts. I saw Grady Nutt at a civic meeting keep a secular audience in stitches for a half hour, and then flip a switch during the last five minutes. Soon hard-hearted men were weeping. The tears never would have flowed without the warm, melting power of laughter.

SHARING HUMOROUS EVENTS WITH THE CONGREGATION

I'm not necessarily a quick-witted person, and I often had to work hard to develop a humorous ending to a story. I stayed alert to humorous events and frequently related funny things that had happened so the whole congregation could share the laughter.

For example, when we were waiting to move into our present church building, the construction was taking so long that some staff members were getting impatient. I instructed our associate ministers to bring a can of spray paint or a magic marker to staff meeting on Monday morning because we were going to take a field trip to the construction site. I would show them where their new office was going to be and I wanted them to write their favorite verse of Scripture on the concrete floor. The floor would soon be carpeted and the Scriptures covered, but they could know they were standing on the Word of God in their office. It was kind of a corny idea—but it caught on, and the staff cooperated.

The children's minister wrote, "Let the little children come unto me" in her office. The music director wrote, "Make a joyful noise to the Lord." I wrote, "Preach the Word in season and out of season." A forty-year-old single woman on staff wrote on her office floor, "If any man would come after me, let him . . . " and "It is not good for a man to be alone." We all burst out laughing when we saw that, and I couldn't wait to tell the whole congregation.

The church not only enjoyed that story, but individual members began to write Scriptures on the floor at the new construction site. Within a few months the entire platform in the sanctuary, the steps leading up to the platform, the center aisle, and the chapel at the opposite end of the lobby were all covered with hundreds of Scripture verses.

SELF-DEPRECATING HUMOR—A WEALTH OF MATERIAL

Dave Stone, my successor, is especially quick-witted and has continued the tradition of laughter. He recently related in a message that he borrowed his neighbor's truck to pick up a large Christmas gift. But when he backed this huge truck into his neighbor's garage he was so worried about not hitting the protruding mirrors against the garage that he backed into the neighbor's car.

At the time his neighbor was attending a party so Dave called his cellphone to tell him the bad news. The neighbor answered his phone, "What is it, Dave?" Then he jokingly added, "You didn't wreck my truck, did you?" Dave said, "No . . . but I did back it into your Lexus. How long have you had that car?" The neighbor paused a moment and said, "It's a new one."

When sharing that incident with the congregation, Dave added, "Really, the guy was so gracious I couldn't believe it. " After pausing another moment he added, "His lawyer has been pretty easy to work with too!"

A lot of humor comes as the result of a preacher being willing to be transparent and laugh at himself. One Sunday night I slept through a church service when I was supposed to be preaching. I'd had a busy weekend and was swamped with responsibility. So I stayed at the church building all Sunday afternoon, finishing up my Sunday evening sermon and writing a funeral sermon for the next day.

The evening service started at 7, and around 6:15 I was ready. But I was also really exhausted. I thought, "I am so worn out! I'm going to lie down on my office floor and rest for a few minutes." As soon as I did I found myself getting drowsy. I thought, "It's okay. If I go to sleep I normally wake up from a nap in ten or fifteen minutes, or I'll hear the people come in, or my wife (or someone who cares) will come in and get me."

I looked out at the congregation. After a long pause I admitted, "Folks, I've got to be honest with you . . ."

The next thing I knew I woke up and thought, "Wow! I thought this was Sunday." Then: "This *is* Sunday!" I looked at my watch and it was 7:35. The service started at 7 and I could hear the congregational singing in the distance. In a panic I wondered, "What should I do?" I quickly went into the restroom, washed my face, and walked confidently into the sanctuary as though I'd been counseling the mayor or someone else important.

Our worship leader had been dragging the song service on, waiting for me to show up, so as soon as I walked in he stopped and nodded to me. I walked toward the platform, not knowing if it was time for me to make announcements or if it was time to preach. I meant to ask, "Where are we in the service?" but instead asked, "Where am I?" The worship leader whispered, "Announcements."

You know how it is when you've just awakened from a nap and your mind is foggy? I looked out at the congregation and couldn't think of a single thing going on in the church all week long to announce. After a long pause I admitted, "Folks, I've got to be honest with you. I went to sleep in the office and I just woke up!"

It took a couple of minutes for the church to settle down, they were laughing so hard. The next morning when I came into the office there was a "Do not disturb" sign on my office door. When I opened it up I discovered that all my office furniture was moved out and all that was in the room was a cot with a teddy bear on it sucking its thumb. Months later at a class social I was given a T-shirt that read "Sleeping Beauty" on the front and "Rip Van Russell" on the back.

To this day people will ask me, "Remember that night when you slept through your sermon?" An associate minister told me a few years later, "I learned so much from that experience. If that had happened to me, I would have been mortified and I would have tried to cover it up. But you were so transparent and just laughed at yourself and as a result the entire congregation enjoyed it."

If you pretend to be perfect people will admire you from a distance—for a while. But they will eventually find out you have feet of clay and regard you as phony. However, if you are transparent about your imperfections and even laugh about them, they will identify with you and love you up close for a long time. So look for the humor in your own mistakes and confess them because "there is a time to laugh."

THE CHURCH IS NOT A CIRCUS: THE DANGER OF EXCESSIVE HUMOR

A word of caution: Laughter is a tool to soften the soil to receive the gospel but it is not an end in itself. John Piper is not a fan of much humor in the pulpit. He fears that laughter promotes an atmosphere that hinders revival. He said, "Laughter seems to have replaced repentance as the goal of some preachers."[3] Admittedly, humor can be taken to the extreme.

If the congregation senses your goal is to be a comedian rather than a communicator of the gospel, you will come across as frivolous and shallow. Phillips Brooks wrote, "The smile that is stirred by true humor and the smile that comes from the mere tickling of the fancy are as different from one another as the tears that sorrow forces from the soul are from the tears that you compel a man to shed by pinching him."

We once hosted Richard Allison, a professional actor who after his conversion to Christ specialized in the dramatic quoting of Scripture. He would memorize long passages and quote them verbatim to the church. He would often use different voices to portray the characters in the biblical story. His presentation was captivating and inspirational.

Richard once quoted the entire ninth chapter of John to our church. He didn't relate anything but the forty-one verses in the Bible, but he used different dialects and voices for Jesus, the disciples, the blind man, his neighbors, and his parents as well as a snarky voice for the Pharisees who investigated the healing.

There was one point during the first service that the congregation burst out laughing when Richard quoted the blind man asking the Pharisees, "Why do you want to hear it again? . . . Do you want to become His disciples too?" It was heartwarming to hear people so "into" Scripture that they could see humor in it.

But when Richard related the same passage the same way the second hour, no one laughed. He didn't skip a beat; he just kept on with the narration. At lunch I asked him, "Richard, did it bother you that no one laughed out loud at that line the second hour?"

He responded, "Oh, not at all. I used to have a drama teacher who taught us, 'Don't listen for the laughter. Listen for the silence.'"

I love to laugh. I love it when the congregation laughs out loud at something genuinely funny. I think it's really healthy. If I could do my ministry again, I'd have the same emphasis. But the finest hour in a church service is when it is absolutely quiet during a pause in the message and all you can hear is the whirring of the air-conditioning fan. At that moment you can feel the presence of the Holy Spirit and the receptivity of softened hearts accepting the truth of God's Word. That's when people are being still and knowing that God is God.

I've concluded that special moment is more likely to happen after the congregation has laughed together because "a cheerful heart is good medicine" (Proverbs 17:22).

II ▶ I WOULD BUILD A TEAM OF HIGHLY QUALIFIED LEADERS AND LEAN ON THEM

Talent wins games, but teamwork and intelligence win championships.

—MICHAEL JORDAN

I once forgot a wedding. It was the worst mistake I ever made in ministry. No preacher ever says to me, "I can top that one!" It doesn't get much worse than that. I had all kinds of excuses: It was on a Saturday, my day off. I had two weddings that day and this was the smaller of the two. The rehearsal had been earlier in the week and not on the previous evening.

But the bottom line is that I really messed up and failed to show up for the most important event in the life of a young couple. I was without excuse. That morning I thought to myself, "I don't have anything today until the wedding tonight at 7:30." So I took my two sons to a ballgame that some of their friends were playing in.

My wife knew I was going to a game but didn't know where.

This was long before cellphones and she had no idea how to reach me. I casually returned home around 1:30 in the afternoon and Judy met me at the door in a panic. "Bob, did you forget that you had a wedding today at one?" My heart sank. It came back to me immediately, and I nearly threw up on the spot.

She said, "They got an associate to perform the wedding." That didn't help at all, since he was actually our elderly custodian who had a ministerial degree in his distant background. This entire episode kept getting worse. I couldn't believe what I had done. How could I be so stupid and so negligent?

I realized I had to apologize as quickly as possible. That old saying came to mind: "If you have a frog to swallow, don't look at it very long." Determined to get it over with, I immediately drove to the church building, anticipating the couple were probably getting their wedding pictures taken.

It's a ten-minute drive from my house to the church, but you wouldn't believe the lies that came to mind on that brief trip. "I got stopped by a stalled train . . . I had a flat tire . . . I saw a vision of a seventy-foot-high Jesus and I was in a trance for two hours." My mind was spinning.

I walked into the auditorium and the entire family was gathered on the platform for pictures. I wanted to turn around and run and never return. The bride spotted me as soon as I walked through the door and called out, "Oh, brother Bob. Thank God! We're so glad you're all right. We were afraid you were in a terrible accident or something. What happened?"

It took every ounce of integrity I could muster to say, "I'm so sorry. I forgot. Please forgive me." To their credit, the family was very gracious to me. But I despised myself that weekend. I wanted to turn back the clock. I wished I could have a do-over. I kept saying to myself, "I don't belong in ministry. Especially this ministry. I should just quit."

That horrible experience forced me to make some dramatic adjustments. First, I had to admit my own weaknesses. I'm not good at administering my own schedule. I'm too much of a people pleaser. I had thirty-two weddings on my calendar that year. When you include numerous rehearsals, rehearsal dinners, and wedding receptions that is beyond overbooking. That's a pathetic need to be liked that's completely out of control.

THE IMPORTANCE OF DELEGATION

On Monday morning I literally took my calendar and laid it in front of my secretary and said, "From now on I want you to run my life. Here are the time slots when I will see people. When anyone asks for an appointment I will say, 'I'd like to see you but my secretary runs my life; please call her.'"

> *God is more likely to work through us if we quit trying so hard to be a hero to everyone.*

I added, "Next year I'm only going to do fifteen weddings, first come, first serve. Channel all other weddings to associate ministers." We also selected a committee to determine which outside speaking engagements I would accept and we developed some reasonable guidelines about how often I would travel.

We arranged a system that on Friday evening my secretary would call my wife and inform her of any scheduled activities on

Saturday since she was not in the office to remind me. My wife would put the Saturday schedule on a Post-it note on the mirror so when I shaved in the morning I would know what I was supposed to do that day. I began to have some margin in my life. There were free weekends. I wasn't so stressed out all the time.

Now it may surprise you that God would use such a "goof-off" to lead a megachurch. But the fact that He did demonstrates that He can use us in spite of weaknesses and character flaws. But He's more likely to work through us if we swallow our pride, admit our shortcomings, gather around us people who have strengths in the areas where we are weak . . . and quit trying so hard to be a hero to everyone.

The apostle Paul wrote, "Do not think of yourself more highly than you ought, but rather think of yourself with sober judgment, in accordance with the faith God has distributed to each of you . . . We have different gifts, according to the grace given to each of us. If your gift is prophesying, then prophecy in accordance with your faith" (Romans 12:3, 6).

So, several years into my ministry, I became intentional about delegating. I determined to focus on my primary gifts (preaching and teaching) and channel other responsibilities to those who were more qualified. The church staff became more important to me. I tried to recruit staff members who were people of integrity and gifted in administration and then trust them to do the job. Today I owe a huge debt of gratitude to a number of wonderful staff people who made me look good.

I'll be the first to tell you that's not always easy. A year after I put a limit on weddings, I was walking through the sanctuary one Saturday morning and saw the custodian setting up for a wedding ceremony. When he told me who was getting married I got really upset because it was the daughter of an influential family I was very close to.

So I went back to my secretary on Monday morning and said, "Look, I know I said just fifteen weddings this year. But when someone like that asks for me, make an exception!" She said coolly, "They didn't ask for you." Wow! Every people pleaser knows how that can hurt.

A lot of the problems we get into in leadership are the result of ego. We like being needed. We like being in control. We like being the center of attention. We like thinking no one can do it as well as we can.

The challenge is to . . .

Delegate even if it hurts your ego. Ask yourself what do you really want? Do you want to impress people or please God?

Delegate in the area of your weakness and stay focused on your strengths. The reason people get burned out is not that they work too hard but they work too hard in an area where they are not gifted. Working in the area of your giftedness energizes you. Working in the area of your weakness drains you.

Delegate and don't micromanage. Gifted people are not going to give their best or stay with you very long if you are always into their details. Surround yourself with talented people and give them space. They may not do it exactly the way you would but just maybe they'll do it better if they have freedom to use their own creativity.

Delegate and help others look good. Give them enough guidelines so they know what's expected, enough resources that they can carry through with their ideas, and enough encouragement that they know when they're doing well.

That's one of the keys to effective leadership. But it requires humility. It requires a willingness to quit trying to impress people and really seeking to please

One preacher told me, "I get the impression in my church that it's my job to cast the vision and the elders' job to stop me."

God. Jesus said, "You know that the rulers of the Gentiles lord it over them, and their high officials exercise authority over them. Not so with you. Instead, whoever wants to become great among you must be your servant, and whoever wants to be first must be your slave" (Matthew 10:25–27).

THE IMPORTANCE OF GOOD LAY LEADERS

I owe a huge debt not only to the church staff but also to the lay leaders of the church who were humble servants. From its inception, Southeast Christian was blessed with a solid core of elders. The church was three years old when the founding minister resigned. The five elders were confident the church, though small at the time, had incredible potential.

When a six-month search for an experienced preacher proved futile, Southeast leaders concluded that God was leading them to a younger minister who would grow with them. They approached the president of Cincinnati Bible College (my alma mater) and asked for the names of recent graduates who had potential. One of them said, "We want to hire a young preacher and we're going to make him successful." I have often thought that phrase "make him successful" ought to be a motto for elders in every church.

In many churches the lay leaders and the minister are at odds with one another. There is often a tug-of-war to see who is really in charge. One preacher told me, "I get the impression in my church that it's my job to cast the vision and the elders' job to stop me." Another preacher emailed me, "I'm looking to relocate. It's a long story but it comes down to this: I can no longer trust my elders. They say one thing and do another, and all to keep one of their number firmly in charge. I can't serve with liars, Bob. I can't worship with those whom I don't respect." Sadly, that's not abnormal.

On the other hand, elders accuse their preacher of being lazy, unethical, controlling, defiant, dishonest, or spiritually immature. One elder joked, "I'm not saying our preacher is a liar, but he sure does remember big!" I received an email from an elder saying, "We discovered our minister is preaching sermons verbatim right off the Internet. We don't expect him to be totally original but we don't want him to be guilty of rank plagiarism either. What should we do?"

THE BIBLICAL HISTORY OF ELDERSHIP

The roots of eldership go back to the story of Moses in Numbers 11. Moses was discouraged because the Israelites were again complaining about their boring diet and questioning Moses's leadership. Moses lost heart. He was ready to quit. He told the Lord, "The burden of leading this people is too much. I would just as soon die as go on."

God came to Moses's rescue by appointing elders to assist him with the task. "The Lord said to Moses: 'Bring me seventy of Israel's elders who are known to you as leaders and officials among the people. Have them come to the tent of meeting, that they may stand there with you. I will come down and speak with you there, and I will take some of the power of the Spirit that is on you and put it on them. They will share the burden of the people with you so that you will not have to carry it alone" (Numbers 11:16–17).

There were two qualifications for the first elders. They were already proven leaders and they were to be anointed by the Holy Spirit. One of the problems in today's churches is that we appoint elders who are not gifted to lead and who don't exhibit the fruit of the Spirit in their lives—and we have trouble.

The responsibility of the first elders was to assist Moses in the mission of getting people to the Promised Land. They were to share the leadership load. Their job wasn't to represent their peer group by passing along criticisms they'd overheard. Their purpose wasn't to double-check the financial status of the Israeli treasury. They were to help Moses carry the burden of leadership so that he didn't have to carry it alone. They helped counsel people. They encouraged Moses. They shared in the decision-making. They defused criticism.

That's the high calling of lay leaders to this day. The elders are to share responsibilities with the up-front leader so they can get as many people to heaven as possible. When Paul met with the elders at Ephesus, a church he established and then shepherded for three years, "he knelt down with all of them and prayed. They all wept as they embraced him and kissed him" (Acts 20:36–37). Theirs wasn't an adversarial relationship, but a shared ministry. That kind of harmonious, caring teamwork creates the foundation for a healthy church.

THE MINISTER AS A PAID ELDER

Paul wrote to a younger preacher, "The elders who direct the affairs of the church well are worthy of double honor, especially those whose work is preaching and teaching. For the Scripture says, 'Do not muzzle the ox while it is treading out the grain,' and 'The worker deserves his wages'" (1 Timothy 5:17–18).

According to that passage the minister is a paid elder. There is an elder whose responsibility is preaching and teaching and who receives a salary so he can give full-time to nurturing the flock. The preacher is not a hired hand, nor is he the chairman of the board of directors. He is one of the elders of the church—but not the only one. In the New Testament there was a plurality of elders who were responsible for directing the affairs of the church. The elder-minister relationship should be one of mutual respect. We are co-laborers with Christ in accomplishing the mission of the church.

I was thankful when I came to Southeast Christian Church that the church bylaws stated that the preacher was considered a paid elder. I was accountable to the other elders, but I had a vote and was regarded as a peer in their discussions. I was given oversight of the paid staff as additional help was employed. Since I was a part of the decision-making body I couldn't blame the elders—I was one of them. That gave me credibility with the congregation. They didn't resent me "pushing my personal agenda" because they knew and respected all the elders.

That solid beginning gave me a respect for the office of elder. I liked having others share the burden with me. I liked not being personally responsible for every decision. I liked not having only my neck on the line for a multimillion-dollar loan! I often discovered the wisdom of the eldership was wiser than my own wisdom. God often worked through the leadership structure He ordained in His Word.

Early in ministry I went to the elders and said, "I'm struggling with time pressure. I'm stretched way too thin. Any suggestions?"

Weaker, carnal elders would have responded, "Well, we all have pressures on our jobs. You're discovering what it's like to work! Welcome to the real world."

Instead our elders responded with understanding and support. They looked for ways to help me carry the burden of all the people. They suggested I quit preaching as many Sunday nights, quit going to all the Sunday school parties, quit going to the hospitals so frequently. Most importantly they suggested I stop doing marital counseling, since I dreaded that part of ministry anyway.

That proved to be a tremendous advantage to me. If people asked me to counsel them in their marriage problems I would say, "I wish I could but the elders have asked me not to do marital counseling. Here's the name of a Christian psychologist who is an excellent marriage counselor. Tell him I sent you."

The elders developed what they at first called a "Discipline Committee" to confront serious conflicts and carnal failures in the

If the only time you see lay leaders is in a meeting, you're seeing them at their worst.

church. Within a few years they wisely changed the name to "The Restoration Committee." That title not only better defined its purpose but improved receptivity on the part of those who were approached. Instead of the preacher having to confront thorny issues, the lay leaders confronted them and I could continue to pastor those who had been "disciplined."

WORKING AS A TEAM

It didn't take me long to recognize the tremendous advantage of having a group of elders who were sharing the burden with me. For that to continue meant that I occasionally had to swallow my pride and be accountable, transparent, and flexible. I had to accept the fact that I didn't always get my way. I wasn't running the show by myself.

It meant I needed to take time to befriend the elders. If the only time you see lay leaders is in a meeting, then you are seeing them at their worst. Meetings are sometimes tense. Leaders are impatient and hope that the meeting will be briefer than normal. That puts people on edge. So it's important that the core leaders be friends with each other . . . and especially friends with the preacher. The minister and his wife can enhance those friendships by opening their home and practicing hospitality with the church leaders. If you eat in one another's homes on occasion, play golf together, attend games together, hunt and fish together, or visit other churches together, you're more likely to develop a healthy appreciation for each other. Then when someone disagrees with your position in a meeting you don't question their integrity because you know their heart.

Most importantly, to have a strong team of leaders around me meant I intentionally helped recruit the smartest, strongest, most spiritual leaders possible to be on the elder board. God told Moses to gather those who "are known to you as leaders and officials." The best church leaders aren't just spiritual; they are powerful personalities in their own circle of influence.

If the preacher is determined to be in charge of everything himself, he will recruit "yes men" or "my guys" for the church board. Or he may talk about "having the right chemistry"—and chemistry is important. But he will soon discover that the most capable leaders don't serve very long because they aren't content to be rubber stamps. Qualified leaders want to make a difference. They want their time to matter and their leadership abilities to be used. If lay leaders sense they're expected just to be cheerleaders for the preacher, they will soon step aside because they want to be in the game and make a difference.

That meant I had to be tough-skinned in meetings and not get rankled when someone disagreed with me or pout or storm out afterward if I didn't get my way. I wanted our elders to be able to treat me like a peer and not be fearful of hurting my feelings.

Once, Jack Coffee, a strong "high D" leader quipped, "Bob, you've brought some silly ideas into this meeting but this may be the worst!" He was only half-joking. I countered, "Now, Jack, that's not true! I've brought some dumber ideas than this! Remember my idea of having the teenage boys drive golf carts all over the parking lot to pick up people? That was a lot worse than this!" The entire eldership, including Jack, burst out laughing and Jack and I went out for ice cream after the meeting. As Oswald Sanders points out, "Willingness to concede error and to defer to the judgment of one's peers increases one's influence rather than diminishes it."[1]

Even in good situations there are conflicts that arise on occasion. Years ago I disagreed with the direction of our missions committee. In my opinion they became too narrowly focused on the recent missions philosophy of the "10-40 window" and were redirecting the majority of our missions funds to reaching "unreached people groups." They were cutting way back on the support of Bible colleges and home missions.

I took our missions director aside, expressed my displeasure, and asked her to return to our previous percentages. She was agreeable, but two days later I got a call from the elder who oversaw the missions department, requesting a meeting. When he came to my office he brought the missions director with him. He said, "Look, we decided in the missions committee that this is the direction we want to take. We have prayed about it. (How do you counter that?) And we don't think you should override our decision."

Then that elder opened the book I had authored, *When God Builds a Church*, and read a paragraph I had written about delegating and not micromanaging. (It was some of the worst advice I ever heard!) He said, "This is really good stuff and you need to follow your own advice."

At the next elders meeting I initiated a serious discussion about where the elders' and the senior minister's authority begins and ends. But even that discussion was congenial because while we disagreed, we understood and respected each other. When that elder died a few years later, I conducted his funeral and was thankful his family considered me one of his closest friends.

I'm convinced the failure to effectively delegate is the primary reason most churches don't grow much beyond 200 people. A talented preacher can be the personal chaplain to a couple hundred people if he really hustles. Most preachers are like Moses in the wilderness, counseling people from dawn to dusk and overextending themselves. Moses's father-in-law, Jethro,

The church can't be viewed as a pyramid with one guy at the top meeting everyone's needs.

confronted him with the truth, "You are wearing yourself out and the people are not getting the best counsel. Appoint capable judges under you and turn this responsibility over to them or you'll not survive" (Exodus 18:17–23).

The church cannot be viewed as a pyramid with one guy at the top meeting everyone's needs, or the base of the pyramid will be limited in size. The church should be envisioned as a circle where the leaders train people to minister to one another. Then there is no limit to the size of the circle that can function effectively.

That's what the apostle Paul suggested in Ephesians 4:11–12: "So Christ himself gave the apostles, the prophets, the evangelists, the pastors and teachers, to equip his people for works of service, so that the body of Christ may be built up." The primary task of the leader is to equip the church to do the work of ministry so we can all "reach unity in the faith and in the knowledge of the Son of God and become mature" (v. 13).

I think there are three major obstacles to effective delegation in the church:

The first is *time demands*. When a little child says, "Mommy, tie my shoe," it's easier to stop and tie the shoe than it is to take time to teach the child to tie it himself. But training the child is the wisest stewardship in the long run. It takes additional time to recruit and train reliable people to do the work of ministry in the church. It's easier and quicker to do it ourselves. But 90 percent of effective administration consists in taking the time to recruit the right volunteers or hire the right staff people and then equip them for service.

The second obstacle is *ego needs*. Preachers are often hesitant to relinquish responsibility because we like being in charge. Or we're afraid the task won't be done as well if we don't do it. We need to seriously ask ourselves, "Why am I here? Am I here to build a personal kingdom or the kingdom of Christ?" That means we can't be control freaks. That means we release control even if it means we don't know everything that's going on.

A woman stopped me in the lobby early one evening and asked, "Do you know where the cancer support group meets?" I told her I didn't but would find out. I checked the schedule at the information desk, found the room, and escorted her to it. I didn't mind telling her that I didn't know where the cancer support group met, but I couldn't quite bring myself to admit to her that I didn't even know we had a cancer support group! But that's okay. Our pastoral care department was doing a good job ministering to people who battled this terrible illness, and I'm thankful for them.

The third obstacle to delegation is the biggest one: *organizational support*. It's one thing for the minister to release responsibility to others and not micromanage; it's another for the elders and congregation to support him behind his back. For example, our elders suggested I cut back on hospital visits and only visit once a week. They assured me they would schedule people with high mercy gifts to visit daily, and that I should visit only the most serious cases.

If someone later complained to an elder, "I was in the hospital for five days and the preacher never came to visit me," the elder needed to protect my back. An incompetent elder would say, "I don't understand that. That's not like Bob. He's normally very good at hospital visitation. I'll check with him and see what happened." Then he'd take me aside on Sunday morning and say, "It might be a good idea for you to call Mrs. Howard. She's a little perturbed that you didn't see her while she was in the hospital."

No! Good elders respond, "Mrs. Howard, we asked Bob not

to make hospital visits but to give his attention to the ministry of the Word of God and prayer. Did someone visit you every day? Remember we've taught you that this church isn't a pyramid with the pastor being your chaplain. It's a circle where we minister to each other." That's a huge difference! And it's rare that elders are willing to give that kind of organizational support.

I took time to inform our people in the new-member classes and occasionally in sermons what they could expect from the preacher. "Because of the size of this church I now only visit people who are terminally ill, so you don't want to see me coming."

One afternoon I was walking toward the intensive care unit at Baptist East hospital. On the way a patient who was a member of our church was standing in the doorway of his room wearing a hospital gown. He saw me coming and exclaimed in mock horror, "Oh no! You're not coming to see me, are you?" When I laughed and assured him I had no idea he was even in the hospital he quipped, "Whew! You made me real nervous. You're kind of like the grim reaper. I don't want you coming to my room!"

Now that's what effective delegation is all about. That's what can happen if we develop a team of highly qualified leaders around us and lean on them for support. And I would do that again.

12▶ I WOULD AVOID GETTING CAUGHT UP IN THE CELEBRITY MENTALITY

You cannot exalt God and yourself at the same time.

—RICK WARREN

The ministry can be a dangerous ego-boost. Especially when the ministry is fruitful, it can produce a false sense of importance in the minister's mind. Every time you get up to preach the spotlight is on you. You are the center of attention. Because of your spiritual position you are loved and revered by many in the congregation.

If you are fairly gifted as a preacher people will heap excessive praise on you for your messages. While we receive our share of criticism, generally speaking, for every critical comment there are twenty encouraging words. "That was a great message." "That was the best sermon on that subject I think I ever heard." "You hit a home run today, preacher!" "You brought out some things about that passage I never thought about before."

Sometimes the praise may be deserved. But let's be honest, no matter how poorly we preach, there will always be compliments from kind souls. Some of them are just flatterers. Some don't know the difference between a good sermon and a poor one. And some are so spiritually hungry they genuinely appreciate those who feed them even a morsel of spiritual bread. The Word of God is so powerful that people are blessed by it regardless of how it's presented.

Some people will say, "Good sermon" because they don't know what else to say. Matt Proctor, president of Ozark Christian College, said as a young preacher he knew he had preached poorly one Sunday but still had several people come through the line and say, "Good sermon." But one veteran attendee was a little more honest. She shook his hand and said, "Nice try." Most people aren't quite that honest, so preachers get complimented a lot.

I once gave the devotional for the Christian golfers on the PGA tour. One excellent player (who will go unnamed) came to the 6:30 service straight from his Wednesday practice round. He was exhausted. Five minutes into my message he nodded off and stayed sound asleep for the entire twenty minutes. After we dismissed he greeted me and said, "Thanks, I got a lot out of that." I'm sure he did.

No matter how poorly we preach, there will always be compliments from kind souls.

It's not just sermons that garner praise. People praise your pastoral care, your helpful counseling, your sound leadership, your ability to relate to older people or to communicate with youth. Since we wear numerous hats, there are many opportunities to do well and to receive praise.

If the church is growing rapidly or gaining favorable attention for its ministry, the preacher receives an inordinate and somewhat dangerous number of accolades. The preacher who stays at one place very long soon becomes kind of a mini-celebrity in the church. Church members want to shake his hand, introduce him to friends, take him out to eat, and even ask him to sign his name in their Bible. Like a quarterback on a winning team, we get more credit than we deserve.

During a period when our church was experiencing explosive growth, I decided I wanted to buy a second car that was more economical. I searched the classified section of our newspaper, found a used car I was interested in, and called for an appointment to see it. The owner gave me his address and told me I could come over anytime the following week after 5 p.m. He would be home and I could examine and test-drive the car.

What I didn't know was the owner was an elder and Sunday school teacher in a local Presbyterian church. He had recently said to a friend, "I'd like to visit Southeast Christian Church sometime and see why that church is growing so rapidly. Next time I'm not scheduled to teach, I'm going to sneak in and observe."

His friend advised him, "Look, if you do visit, don't sign anything. The way that church is growing they probably have an aggressive calling program and someone will be knocking on your door the following week."

Well, it just so happened that the week I phoned about the car was the week he came to visit our church. On Monday evening around 5:30 he looked out his kitchen window and there I came strolling down his sidewalk. He blurted out to his wife, "Wow! That guy is phenomenal! I visit his church one time, there are thousands of people in attendance, I don't sign anything and the next night he comes to visit me. No wonder that church is growing like they are."

As I approached the front door, I said to my wife, "Don't tell him I'm a preacher. I want to dicker a little on the price of this car." He opened the door and greeted me warmly, "Bob Russell! Come on in!" I paid full price for the car.

The preacher often gets more credit than he deserves and more attention than his position merits, not only in the church but also in the surrounding community. When you go out to eat or attend a ballgame people notice you and call out to you. Since I preached in Louisville for a long time, I became more and more recognized in the community.

I have season tickets to University of Louisville football games. Many of my friends who are season-ticket holders complain that the profanity in their section is so bad that they can't bring their kids to the game. But I don't remember the last time I heard profanity in the section where I sit. It is the most spiritual section in Papa John's stadium, and I don't hesitate to take my grandchildren to the games. Knowing there's a preacher in the section has nearly eliminated foul language.

THE DANGER OF PRAISE

All that can be pretty heady stuff and the preacher can begin to believe his own press clippings. But Proverbs 16:18 warns, "Pride goes before destruction, a haughty spirit before a fall."

Former North Carolina Senator John Edwards admitted to committing adultery with a campaign worker in 2006. He said, "I made a serious error in judgment. In the course of several campaigns

I started to believe that I was special and became increasingly ego-centric and narcissistic."[1]

That can happen to ministers also. We start believing we are someone special. We think we're above the rules and become easy targets for the enemy. The apostle Paul warned about preaching to others and then becoming disqualified for the prize (1 Corinthians 9:27). We can all list well-known preachers who fell victim to an affair, pornography, embezzlement, drugs, or alcoholism primarily because of arrogance. A haughty spirit went before a fall.

Admittedly, I had to battle pride since things went well in my ministry. Over the years Southeast Christian Church grew by hundreds, then thousands. When I retired we were averaging over 18,000 in attendance, baptizing over a thousand a year. More and more people came to our leadership conference to learn keys to church growth.

But for the most part I think I avoided the celebrity mentality. I considered it a compliment when someone would say to me, "You don't act like a minister of a large church." Our local newspaper did an article about me that they headlined, "Just Plain Bob," noting that I didn't demand titles or special privileges. I hope I didn't take pride in that unassuming reputation, but I do have to admit I appreciated hearing it. I once read that "humility is a slippery virtue—once you think you've got it, you've lost it."

> *I had to battle pride since things went well in my ministry.*

While he preached for The Moody Church in Chicago, Harry Ironside realized he was being tempted by pride since the church's 4,000-seat auditorium was always full for his sermons. He concluded he should do something humbling to battle the temptation. So Dr. Ironside answered a help-wanted ad and spent an entire day walking the streets of downtown Chicago carrying a sandwich board promoting a local restaurant.

When he came home later that evening he was totally exhausted. When he took off his shoes and collapsed into a chair he said his first thought was, "That's the most humiliating thing I've ever done in my life!" Then his second thought was, "I'll bet there's not another preacher in Chicago who would be willing to do what I did today."[2]

AVOIDING ARROGANCE

Humility is indeed a slippery virtue and takes constant vigilance to maintain. Since the Word of God says, "God opposes the proud but shows favor to the humble" (James 4:6), here are several exercises that ministers can practice to avoid arrogance:

Remember your roots. "Brothers and sisters, think of what you were when you were called. Not many of you were wise by human standards; not many were influential; not many were of noble birth. But God chose the foolish things of the world to shame the wise; God chose the weak things of the world to shame the strong. God chose the lowly things of this world and the despised things—and the things that are not—to nullify the things that are, so that no one may boast before him" (1 Corinthians 1:26–29).

I grew up in the country milking cows every morning. My home church had less than a hundred people. I was so insecure as a boy I was terrified to read in front of a small group. I graduated in the middle of my high school class of sixty. Without Jesus Christ I am a nobody.

Intentionally give glory to God when people praise you. Don't get obnoxious with your humility. The "Oh, don't thank me, thank Jesus" brand of fake modesty makes everyone feel uncomfortable. But we can say, "That's so nice of you to say so. Thanks. God has been really good to me." Or, "Isn't it amazing how the Holy Spirit works through the Bible?" Or, "That means a lot coming from you. But I had an awful lot of help, believe me." Then the person giving the compliment feels appreciated, and both of you are reminded that the ultimate glory goes to God.

Be accountable to someone who will tell you the truth and ask tough questions. Some guys benefit from an accountability group. I'm not as high on structured accountability groups as some, because I've witnessed deceptive people hoodwink even those who thought they were totally transparent. But preachers need to be accountable to someone. We need elders or a board of directors who will ask tough questions, check expense accounts, listen for doctrinal deviations, and watch for inappropriate encounters or prideful attitudes.

Spend significant time with friends and family members who aren't overly impressed with you. The church members I enjoyed being with the most were those who treated me like an ordinary human being, not a celebrated preacher. I had enough people telling me I was special; I needed some truth-tellers who teased me and roughed me up on occasion.

My wife and family have always been more than happy to serve in that role. My wife never put me on a pedestal. One evening just minutes before I was leaving to preach at our church's leadership conference, Judy asked me to vacuum the family room since guests were coming over after the meeting. She didn't seem too impressed that several thousand church leaders had driven miles to hear me preach in a few minutes. I swept the floor.

My sons and grandchildren don't treat me like a celebrity. After hearing people praise me they delight in bringing me back down to reality a few minutes later. The past three Christmases my grandchildren have given me humorous gifts reminding me of who I really am. One year they gave me a cufflink box. When it's opened, a recording intones, "You're the best, Bob . . . You're one of a kind, Bob . . . You're wonderful, Bob." When I opened it and listened we all burst into hilarious laughter, because I knew it was a subtle reminder that at home I was just Pop—the old guy who falls asleep on the couch and snores.

Last year they gave me an ice cube tray that makes ice cubes that spell the name "Bob." "Here, Pop, now you can have your own individual ice cubes in case you forget who you are." Just a few days ago they gave me a sweatshirt that reads, "This is what an awesome Bob looks like." We all laugh at these gifts because we know they are given tongue in cheek. Their sarcasm and the authenticity of our relationships help keep my feet on the ground and my head out of the clouds.

Embrace the humbling experiences God brings into your life. Instead of resenting embarrassing moments, welcome them as God-given reminders of your humanity and laugh at yourself. Years ago I preached a one-week revival meeting in Lawrenceburg, Indiana, an hour and a half drive upriver from Louisville. I drove up each night, preached and then drove home.

There was an eight-year-old boy in that church who thought I was the greatest. His parents told me he just idolized me. He wanted to be a preacher just like me someday, so after each service he would come and stand by me and look at me with an admiration that, frankly, was a little embarrassing. He was really excited because on Thursday night I wasn't going to drive back to Louisville, I was staying at his house and sleeping in his room. He couldn't wait.

I tried not to let him down. Before we went to sleep we had prayer together and we talked for a few minutes. He was in the upper bunk, I was in the lower bunk. Then all of a sudden after a few minutes of silence I heard him whimpering, almost sobbing. I asked, "Timmy, what's wrong?" He burst out, "You sound like a pig!" I realized I had fallen asleep and had started snoring. I laughed and tried to calm him down a little, but he would have none of it. He grabbed his pillow and scurried to his parents' bedroom and spent the rest of the night with them. On Friday night of the meeting he would have nothing to do with me . . . the little wimp!

That was humbling. I went from being the next best thing since the apostle Paul to being an old snoring hog in a few seconds. God will bring people and experiences into your life that will keep you humble. Instead of resenting those people, welcome them, laugh about them—or, better still, listen to them. They may be just what you need to keep you from becoming arrogant and self-centered.

Stay close to Christ. The Scripture records that every time someone saw the Lord in His glory, their first reaction was fear and self-loathing. "Depart from me for I am a sinful man, O Lord," said Simon Peter. "I am a man of unclean lips and dwell in the midst of people with unclean lips," Isaiah cried.

The closer you are to Christ, the more aware you are of your own sinfulness and inadequacy. That's why the apostle Paul wrote, "I am the worst of sinners" (1 Timothy 1:15) and "May I never boast except in the cross of our Lord Jesus Christ" (Galatians 6:14).

There's a balance that's needed here. Some go to the extreme and don't take advantage of the leadership role God has given. When Joseph was promoted from the prison to the palace in Egypt, he accepted the perks that came with the position and used them to lead effectively. He wore Pharaoh's signet ring, linen robe, and gold necklace. He rode in Pharaoh's impressive chariot with its security personnel. He didn't confuse humility with reluctance. He recognized that God had gifted him and equipped him to lead.

When Esther was selected as the queen, she didn't refuse to reign or take advantage of her lofty position. She acknowledged that God had brought her into the kingdom "for such a time as this" and used her influence to save her people.

A general needs to wear additional stars. The orchestra director needs to be the only one with a baton. The President needs to be surrounded by Secret Service. There's a place for proper dignity, authority symbols, and leadership perks. The High Priest in the Old Testament days was to wear distinctive clothing. The Bible does say we are to respect those who are over us in the Lord (1 Thessalonians 5:12). A local preacher needs to be esteemed and loved. The idea of leading from behind is mostly a myth.

Spiritual leaders are most effective when they feel comfortable in their own skin and yet lead with a servant's heart. The great stage and film star Sir Laurence Olivier was once asked what it took to be a great actor. He responded, "Humility enough to prepare and confidence enough to perform." That's the balance that's needed in ministry. Enough holy fear to remain dependent on God every day, yet enough confidence in our divine call that we remain strong and courageous no matter how challenging the assignment.

"All of you, clothe yourselves with humility toward one another, because, 'God opposes the proud but shows favor to the humble.' Humble yourselves, therefore, under God's mighty hand, that he may lift you up in due time. Cast all your anxiety on him because he cares for you" (1 Peter 5:5–7).

13▶ I WOULD STAY WITH WHAT WORKS AND NOT GET TOO QUICKLY SWEPT UP IN THE LATEST FADS

Much of the social history of the Western world over the past three decades has been a history of replacing what worked with what sounded good.

—THOMAS SOWELL

A few years before my parents died I went back to my hometown in Pennsylvania for a nostalgic visit. One night before I went to bed I did something I had done scores of times as a teenage boy. I sat at the kitchen table and ate a bowl of Wheaties. That was a common practice for me when I was in high school, and it brought back a lot of memories. Same taste, same size box, same logo, same slogan, "Breakfast of Champions."

However, I discovered something that evening. Mickey Mantle's picture wasn't on the front of the Wheaties box anymore. I think at the time it was Tiger Woods. General Mills recognizes they have a great product in Wheaties, but to continue to successfully market their product their packaging has to change.

The same is true with the ministry of a church. Our product doesn't change. Jesus Christ is the same yesterday, today, and forever. The human heart hasn't changed; people still need forgiveness of sin, the hope of eternal life, and an ultimate purpose for every day. We don't need to change the gospel, but the packaging has to change frequently.

There's an old slogan most of us have quoted often because it sums up the challenge of Christian leadership: "Methods are many, principles are few. Methods always change, principles never do." Effective church leaders have to change methods at the appropriate time. That's not easy to do because people resist change. They don't want to get out of their comfort zone so they complain about or criticize almost every change. They recall previous changes that didn't work. They resist change even when it's obviously for the best.

A preacher I hadn't seen in two years asked almost immediately, "What are you doing that's new and different?"

Jesus said, "You don't put new wine in old wineskins." Culture changes. Personnel age. Competition improves. Programs have a shelf life. In this rapidly changing environment, we must change methods or we will die. Show me a church that's programming like it did fifty years ago and I'll show you a church that's dead—or on life support. Will Rogers once said, "You can be on the right track but you'll get run over if you're standing still."

AN OBSESSION WITH CHANGE

However, it seems to me there's almost an obsession among some church leaders these days with dramatic, frequent changes. They have an intense desire to be cutting-edge. Like the Athenians, they do nothing but talk about and listen to the latest ideas (Acts 17:21). They chase after the creative and the unique. A preacher, whom I had not seen in two years, asked almost immediately, "What are you doing that's new or different?"

A speaker at a recent conference began his message by asking everyone to take out their cellphones. Everyone knew the drill. We expected him to say, "Turn off your cellphone so there won't be interruptions." Instead he said, "Be sure your cellphone is on. Now if I say anything worth repeating, text it instantly to five minister friends. Let's get this message out."

Everyone attending the conference really liked that because it was a good example of using technology to our advantage. It was relating to the culture. It was innovative. That's good. Culture does change, and we need to adapt so we can be relevant.

But if we're too obsessed with new and creative ideas we can wind up reinventing church every four or five years and lose leadership credibility. People eventually dismiss our excitement about a new direction as another passing fancy and don't embrace the program. Charles Spurgeon had it right years ago when he said, "He who marries today's fad will soon be a widow."

For example, a veteran school principal told me the education system has chased after so many fads in recent years that his peers just shake their heads in disgust at the latest innovation that they're promised is going to transform education. First, it was government-mandated busing that was going to solve racial tension. Then it was the state-sponsored lottery that was supposed to cure all financial issues. Then it was new math that was going to simplify mathematics. That was followed by an exaggerated emphasis on positive reinforcement that promised to solve behavioral problems. Then there was an arbitrary quota system and politically correct terminology promoting diversity. Now it's gender-neutral language and restrooms to assure everyone is valued. He says only the young and naïve teachers get excited about the new ideas. Most just snicker up their sleeve and shrug it off.

To paraphrase Thomas Sowell, American economist and political philosopher, as I look back I'm thankful I wasn't too quick too replace what was working with "what sounded good."

A more serious danger of being overly focusing too much on being cutting-edge is that we are tempted to adjust the message to relate to the culture. We can work so hard to understand how the world thinks that we wind up saying what the world wants to hear. Since the premier virtue of this age is tolerance, there's a temptation for us to shout grace and whisper repentance. We rationalize that we're just relating to the culture but in reality we're saying what itching ears want to hear.

DISCERNING BETWEEN A
PASSING FAD AND A PERMANENT TREND

When evaluating potential change, a Christian leader needs the perception to discern between a permanent trend and a passing fad. During the past fifty years there have been trends that the church needed to embrace. We changed translations from the King

James to the New International Version. We moved from using an organ and piano to using guitars and drums. We moved from a choir to a praise team. We changed from using hymnals to projecting words on the screen. We dropped Sunday night church services in favor of small groups meeting in homes.

During the same time period there have been some passing fads also. In the late sixties the cutting-edge program was a bus ministry. Churches bought a fleet of buses and sent them all over the county, picking up children from up to an hour away, and trucked them to church in hopes their parents would follow. That proved to be impractical, disruptive, and ineffective.

Then there was the seeker-sensitive emphasis. We were encouraged to design the Sunday worship service to reach the unbeliever. Sing just one song a week, since the seeker doesn't relate to congregational singing. Eliminate special music and have a drama every week instead (which often became little more than a camp skit) because the visitor relates to the arts. Then it was the elimination of all religious symbols. Don't put a cross anywhere on the building because the cross sends mixed signals. Make the building as business-friendly as possible.

That was followed by the accountability fad. Every believer must be in a weekly small group where tough questions are asked and people are honest and transparent. While accountability groups have value, there were also serious loopholes and they can't be arbitrarily forced on people. I haven't heard as much about accountability groups in recent years.

One of the ongoing challenges for every leader is to discern between a passing fad and a permanent trend. I think I avoided the extremes of refusing to change at all and the opposite extreme of getting caught up too quickly in the latest fad and having to reverse gears every few years.

Sometimes that meant enduring criticism that I wasn't relevant. Sometimes it meant our church's leadership conference wasn't cutting-edge enough to draw big crowds. Sometimes it meant tolerating the not-so-well-disguised exasperation of young staff members who had just returned from the latest conference and were confident they knew more about leading the church than I did.

Sometimes it meant disregarding the dire predictions of futurists. Some "experts" who have never built a church analyze statistics and make dogmatic predictions about the future that can intimidate uncertain leaders into hasty action. For example, fifteen years ago we were told that the megachurch was going to be a dinosaur in a decade. That hasn't come true at all.

Bernard Baruch was an American financier who made millions on investments in the mid-1900s. He once quipped, "A financial consultant is someone who thinks he knows more about money than us that has it." I sometimes feel that way about some church consultants. They think they know more about what it takes to build the church than ministers who have actually done it.

Think of the stylistic issues in today's church. What's a passing fad? What's a permanent trend? Casual dress, darkened auditoriums, preaching without notes, organic sermons, one-point sermons (divided five different ways), and the pulpit replaced with a round table and a stool. Calling Christians "Christ followers" and the senior minister the "lead pastor"; no invitation at the end of the sermon; the avoidance of patriotism or any display of the flag. Satellite churches, the emphasis on the arts, ZIP code pastors, missional churches verses attractional churches, building new buildings versus renovating supermarkets, more emphasis on discipleship, less on mass evangelism—are these passing fads or permanent trends?

The church has to change methods or we'll become a relic of the past. On the other hand, we can create havoc in the church by insisting on "keeping up with the times" when in reality we're chasing another passing whim and just trying to be cool. John Piper wrote, "If you crave to be cool you will eventually compromise truth. The god of this age will not allow truth to be cool for long."

BE PATIENT

I would offer three suggestions on this subject. First, unless you sense a divine imperative to be a pioneer, be patient. God does anoint some to innovate, but don't be a groupie to every new idea that comes along. Be content to let others pave the way. Learn from their mistakes and profit from their successes. Be smart enough to ask yourself the questions, "Now just where is this idea working effectively? Will it work here? And have we laid the proper groundwork?" Do your homework and seek wise counsel before dragging your congregation into still another hip idea that is long on promise and short on delivery.

Dave Stone and the elders at Southeast Christian have established three of the healthiest satellite churches I know of anywhere. But they weren't pioneers in that field. They took their time, studied best practices, and learned from the admitted miscues of other churches. Over the past six years Southeast Christian systematically launched three multisite churches that each began with around 1,500 people. Each congregation is well staffed and has an adequate facility.

A decade ago some might have accused Southeast of not being on the cutting edge of the multisite ministry, but by taking their time they avoided the loss of finances and leadership credibility that sometimes comes from jumping on the bandwagon of the latest fad.

I like the droll humor of comedian Stephen Wright. One of my favorite quips of his is, "The early bird catches the worm; but it's the second mouse that gets the cheese!" Enough said.

STAY WITH WHAT WORKS

Secondly, stay with what works. Don't change just to be cutting edge. What doesn't work well someplace else may still be effective for you. So stay with it and don't apologize for it if it's working in your situation.

My friend Cam Huxford has led in building one of the most effective ministries in the South. Savannah Christian Church has grown to nearly 10,000 people. Every year they conduct an old-fashioned "Journey to Bethlehem" that's held out of doors and inspires thousands. A fellow minister asked, somewhat condescendingly, "Are you still doing that old program?" Cam confidently responded, "Yep! And it's still attracting 30,000 people every year."

BE CONFIDENT IN THE GOSPEL

Thirdly, put your confidence in and invest the majority of your time in the study of the Word of God and not investigating all the latest religious fads. "Whoever invokes a blessing in the land will do so by the one true God" (Isaiah 65:16). We bless our territory by proclaiming the truth of God's Word.

The use of cutting-edge methods is, in my opinion, less than 10 percent of the basis of a healthy ministry. Ninety percent of your influence in the future will depend on whether or not you can take the bread of life and feed it to people. Can you make God's Word understandable, practical, and inspirational? If so, God will honor that because "the word of God is alive and active. Sharper than any double-edged sword . . . it judges the thoughts and attitudes of the heart" (Hebrews 4:12).

Five years ago Bo Chancey accepted the call to an outstanding church in Manchester, New Hampshire. The Manchester Christian Church was averaging about a thousand people at the time. That was almost unheard of in our movement. The East Coast is considered hard soil, but this church had expanded its influence and reached hundreds of people.

The previous minister and worship leader had teamed up to steadily build a dynamic church based on the seeker-sensitive philosophy. They used cutting-edge music, relevant programming, and hip terminology and erected a building with no cross or religious symbols. God honored their efforts and Manchester Christian became one of the largest in that region.

When that minister retired, Bo Chancey was hired as the new, younger pastor. Bo is from Texas. He went to Bible college in the Midwest. He admits he looks a lot like Opie Taylor from Andy Griffith's Mayberry. Some leaders in New Hampshire were worried that this "hayseed" wouldn't understand their sophisticated, contemporary ministry.

Bo, who is sharp as a tack, announced one of his first sermon series would be "Jesus: Lord and Savior." A staff member cautioned him, "I don't think our congregation will relate to 'Lord and

Savior'—we speak of Jesus as leader and healer." Bo said, "Really? Then I'll take thirty minutes in the first sermon to explain it to them. I think they're astute enough to grasp it."

Bo just started preaching expository sermons from the Bible. He suggested, "I think I'd like to ask people to stand in the morning worship service if they would like to be prayed for." "Oh, no," a staff member objected. "These people are too sophisticated for that. That will make them feel uncomfortable." Bo said, "Let's try it."

Prayer time became a popular feature in the church service as the congregation started to humble themselves and pray for one another. Bo authored a book, *Pray for One*, in which he relates how he encouraged his people to pray for someone they knew who was lost. What seemed to be taboo terminology and "religious" programming was working—even in New Hampshire.

Eventually Bo Chancey decided he'd like to put up a cross outside their building. There were objections from some long-term leaders: "Many will find that offensive—it's an old, ineffective symbol."

The secret to spiritual power is not being cool but exalting Christ.

Bo said, "Look, we're a church. We're not trying to sneak up on anybody. We're inviting people to come to the cross. Jesus promised, 'If I be lifted up I'll draw all men to me.' We don't need to apologize for that."

Wisely, Bo retained much of the cutting-edge methodology he inherited and even added to it. But he hasn't been afraid to walk in some old paths either. The Manchester Christian Church has grown to nearly 3,000 people in five years. It has more than tripled in attendance. That's incredible growth and influence in a medium-sized, sophisticated city on the East Coast.

If you're a preacher, I would challenge you to: preach the Word. Revere Jesus Christ. Lift up the cross. Honor family values. The secret to spiritual power is not being cool but exalting Christ. "See that what you heard from the beginning remains in you. If it does, you also will remain in the Son and in the Father. And this is what he promised us—eternal life" (1 John 2:24–25).

14 ▶ I WOULD STAY IN ONE PLACE FOR FORTY YEARS AND MOVE TO A NEW CHAPTER WHILE I WAS STILL YOUNG ENOUGH TO EMBRACE THE OPPORTUNITY

So all you boomers just breaking into Medicare, gird your loins . . . Fix your eyes on Jesus' face at the finish line. There will be plenty of time for R and R in the resurrection. For now, there's happy work to be done.

—JOHN PIPER

When I accepted the ministry at Southeast Christian Church in Louisville, Kentucky, I had no idea I would stay at the same church for forty years. In the back of my mind I anticipated staying in

Louisville for five or six years and then returning to Pennsylvania or someplace on the East Coast where our brotherhood of churches were few and struggling.

But I soon discovered that Southeast Christian was a great church that God thrust upon me. And I knew a good thing when I was in the middle of it. This church had qualified leadership, an ideal location, and ample resources in a spiritually malnourished area.

Besides, I liked living in Louisville. I discovered it's a great place to live and raise a family. In my opinion one of the wisest things a young preacher can do is to fall in love with his community. There is no perfect place, but it boosts the spirit of your people to know that you focus on the positives and like the apostle Paul, you have learned to be content wherever you are.

It became obvious that God was able to do considerably more than I ever asked or imagined. In 1966 when I first started, the church consisted of 120 people, meeting in the basement of a house. The first church building was already under construction when I arrived. When we occupied the 550-seat sanctuary six months later we doubled in attendance the first year. Within five years we went to two worship services and were averaging more than 600 in worship, which was considered a large church in that day.

Since the church was doing so well I received several requests from other churches, asking me to consider becoming their minister. I'd listen to their appeal, churn about it, pray over the decision, and eventually decide to stay where I was. On those few occasions when I seriously entertained an invitation to go elsewhere, I found myself distracted from my main focus—and that wasn't healthy.

One day a pulpit committee, representing what was generally considered to be one of the most "prestigious" churches in our movement, asked me to interview with them. Their elderly minister had retired and they decided to call a younger man whom they felt could rejuvenate their historic church. I was in my early thirties and was very flattered. This would be a "step up the ladder" in the eyes of many. The church also paid their minister very well.

As I churned over what to do, I shared my opportunity with an older, wiser minister. Without much thought he asked me a penetrating question: "Why would you want to go to a church with a great past when you're at a church with a great future?"

> *Without much thought he asked me a penetrating question: "Why would you want to go to a church with a great past when you're at a church with a great future?"*

That phrase stayed with me for the rest of my ministry. Southeast had great potential. Why should I leave when things were going well and I was happy? I wasn't supposed to be in ministry for "prestige" or financial gain. I had been called to win people to Christ and build up the kingdom of God.

At that point I decided as long as I was happy and the church was doing well, I wouldn't even consider the idea of leaving. When someone called with a new ministry challenge, I immediately responded, "Thank you. I'm honored by your request but I'm not even entertaining the thought of leaving at this time. Let me give you a couple of names of guys who might be interested."

If we have no intention of leaving, it's not fair to a pulpit committee to string them along just to see what may be offered. This is not to say that every minister should stay at the same church for a lifetime. Sometimes God's call to a new ministry is obvious. Sometimes the minister needs a fresh challenge or it's best for his family to relocate. Sometimes ministers are asked to leave by the congregation because the lay leaders are dissatisfied with the lack of progress.

THE POSITIVES OF A LONG-TERM MINISTRY

I chose to remain at Southeast for forty years and discovered there are numerous advantages that accompany a long-term ministry. Stability for the congregation, expanded influence in the community, and in-depth pastoral relationships are a few of the benefits. I was blessed to perform wedding ceremonies for young people decades after marrying their parents. I was almost an honorary family member to several in our congregation.

One of the biggest benefits of staying in one place for a long time was the blessing it was to my children. My two sons had deep roots in the church and in Louisville. They loved the church and their hometown. They were spared the insecurity of not knowing where they were going to school the next year, as well as the potentially wounding experiences that many preacher's kids experience in a contentious or unstable church. The fact that both my sons and all seven of my grandchildren are actively involved in the church today can largely be attributed to the steadfast and positive spiritual environment they experienced growing up.

At leadership conferences I often pointed out that 95 percent of Southeast Christian Church was great. It's one of the best churches I know. But about 4 percent is not so hot. And 1 percent is downright nasty. My challenge, as a leader, is that 50 percent of my time is focused on trying to correct the 5 percent that's negative, and I lose the big picture. I have to constantly remind myself to think about that which is noble, right, and admirable.

Even more important than keeping the big picture myself is to make sure my children do the same. They didn't need to hear about the negative 5 percent. They needed to hear about the 95 percent that was positive. Preachers can skew their children's perspective of the church by airing all their complaints at the Sunday dinner table. My son Rusty is now preaching in Florida. My son Phil is a deacon at Southeast Christian Church. I can't remember them ever saying anything negative about the direction of our church—even after my retirement. I'm thankful for that. I hope they caught that spirit from their parents.

One of the richest blessings of a long-term ministry is to witness the harvest of seeds that were sown, decades before. A Crisis Pregnancy Center that began on a shoestring now saves hundreds of babies and ministers to a host of troubled women every year. A Christian school that began meeting in our Sunday school classrooms now has three campuses and is the largest Christian school in the nation with 3,000 students.

A ministry can recover from a mistake much easier than it can recover from stagnation.

A mission program that began with a mustard seed–sized budget now annually exceeds $10 million and sponsors an annual Global Medical Missions Conference.

It's rewarding to hear positive reports from new church plants and to witness the impact of hundreds of young men and women who grew up in our church and now have gone into ministry and mission fields. It's gratifying to see people who have been baptized at our church grow to maturity and start ministries to abused women, oversees orphanages, an inner-city medical clinic, a Christian retreat center, and a production studio making instructional videos and full-length Christian movies. Those are noteworthy harvests that are especially gratifying in a long-term ministry because we are privileged to witness the fruit of our ministry firsthand.

THE NEGATIVES OF A LONG-TERM MINISTRY

There are some dangers as well. A preacher who stays in one place for years has to guard against complacency. There's a temptation to coast because the congregation is comfortable with you. We've learned how to cut corners and how to recycle sermons and programs without much effort. When we become at ease in Zion, soon the entire church becomes lethargic and resistant to change. It's my observation that a ministry can recover from a mistake much easier than it can recover from stagnation. And the man who oversees a period of decline is almost never the man to revitalize the work.

If a preacher stays in one place for very long he has to accept the fact that he will be taken for granted sometimes. A guest speaker gets praised for saying the same thing you've said repeatedly. A new preacher experiences a honeymoon period where he can do no wrong. But if he stays for a few years, the romance fades and the nitty-gritty of reality sets in. A prophet is not without honor except in his own country, and there are times when familiarity breeds contempt in ministry. It's normal to be taken for granted in a lasting marriage and it's normal in a long ministry.

A preacher who stays in one place also has to accept the unpleasant fact that there will probably be a loss of friendships along the way. I'm thankful for friendships that have lasted for fifty years. But I've lost a few too. Some friends died. Some moved away. The losses that hurt the most were those who left because of a disagreement with me, or entanglement with the world.

It's painful when friends tell you, "You know we love you but we're going to look for another church." It hurts when the people who start out climbing the mountain with you aren't there at the peak to rejoice with you and enjoy the view at the top. We've accepted the loss of some friendships but really cherish the ones that have been through the entire experience with us.

PASSING THE BATON

After being the preacher at Southeast for almost thirty-five years, I began thinking about when and how to gracefully step aside. A father who really cares about his family has to think about life insurance—"What happens if I'm taken out of the picture?" A preacher who really cares about his flock has to think about what will happen to the church if he dies or becomes too old to lead effectively anymore.

In the spring of 1999 I read an eye-opening book by Joel Gregory entitled *Too Great a Temptation*.[1] It presented Gregory's perspective of the botched transition at First Baptist Church in Dallas, Texas, which had been a flagship church in its denomination. The book showed how an established church can quickly become divided and lose its testimony if the baton isn't passed prudently from a long-term minister to his successor.

Gregory's book sobered me. I thought, "We can't allow that to happen at Southeast Christian. This ministry is too important for my ego to get in the way of its future. Whatever the elders and I need to do to see that this work continues at its peak effectiveness, we need to do."

I gave each of our elders a copy of Gregory's book. After they read it we had a frank discussion about the impending transition. Needless to say that was a solemn, no-nonsense meeting. I was not quite sixty years old at the time, but we all recognized the long-term implications and its necessity. The elders eventually challenged me to return from my next study-break with a skeleton transition plan they could consider.

In fall 1999 I presented a four-step transition plan. (Details are available in the eBook *Transition Plan*.)

(1) I would step down from leading Southeast sometime between 2006 and 2008.

(2) Dave Stone, who had been serving as an associate preaching pastor, would become the senior minister. Until my retirement was final, Dave's preaching assignments would increase one Sunday each year.

(3) We would begin an immediate search for a third teaching minister who would share the pulpit with Dave following my retirement. (Three years later this proposal led to the hiring of Kyle Idleman, age twenty-six, who immediately began preaching ten weekends a year.)

(4) Following my retirement I would absent myself from all worship services at Southeast for at least a year. This would signal to the church that my leadership role was over and would free my

successors to make changes they deemed necessary without me "looking over their shoulder."

I did not include anything about financial benefits in my recommendations. I trusted the Lord would direct the elders to provide. I am very grateful to the compensation committee for their extreme generosity to me in the retirement package they provided. It was much more than fair and I will be forever grateful for their kindness.

It didn't take very long for me to choose the 2006 date for my retirement. I reasoned that I would celebrate my fortieth anniversary as minister on the first Sunday of July 2006, and that should be my final day. Moses led Israel for forty years and then God chose to replace him with Joshua. Forty years was long enough for me. I wanted to go out when I was still competent, and I didn't want to spend my final years wondering if people were questioning how long I was going to hang on. Besides, we now had two younger associates, Dave and Kyle, who were eager and capable of leading the church.

We announced to the congregation five years out what the plan would be. That announcement served as a reminder to them that Christ was the head of the church, not the preacher. It answered their questions about the upcoming direction and gave additional credibility to Dave Stone.

I walked away on the second Sunday of July 2006 and rejoiced. An observation I had read a few years earlier helped: "A ministry isn't really so hard to give up if you remember that it wasn't really yours in the first place."

I now go back to visit Southeast worship services ten or twelve weekends a year and return to preach there about once a year.

When Dave or Kyle walk to the platform to preach, not one time have I thought, "I wish I were preaching today." They do a terrific job, and I'm glad I don't have that intense pressure anymore.

The church has done extremely well under the new leadership. Southeast has established three very effective satellite churches and the overall average attendance at our four campuses now exceeds 23,000. The attendance is just one measure of the church's progress in recent years. The number of conversions and transformed lives, the expanded missions outreach, the influence in the community, the overall impact for Christ continues to give evidence of God's blessing. I rejoice that the church is now totally debt free.

At the first elders' meeting after I left, Matt Chalfant, chairman of the elders, announced, "We're not going to have a typical meeting tonight. Let's go down to the sanctuary together." There in that empty auditorium were two special chairs, one on each side of the platform. Dave Stone was asked to sit in one; Kyle Idleman was instructed to sit in the other.

Matt said, "Guys, this is where you're going to be preaching week by week from now on. We're going to have a prayer session tonight asking for God's blessing and direction on your ministry." For the next half hour, one by one the elders stood behind those two ministers, laid hands on them and prayed for God's anointing, God's protection, God's wisdom to guide them.

Then when the elders had finished praying, unbeknownst to Dave and Kyle, some of their closest friends had been invited to join the prayer service. The ministers would feel a hand on their shoulder and then hear a familiar, friendly voice behind them praying for God's blessing and affirming their confidence in them.

Dave and Kyle did not know about the next step either. Their families had traveled secretly to be with them on this significant night of prayer. When their friends had finished praying and embracing them, Dave and Kyle would feel another set of hands on their shoulder and then hear the voice of their dad, their mother, and their siblings one by one praying for them.

The tears flowed. The Holy Spirit came down. And it's no wonder God has continued to honor the leadership and ministry of that church.

Two weeks before my retirement the chairman of the elders was buttonholed by an older, confrontational member. "I want to know what you guys are going to do when the man who established and built this

> *For a transition to be successful, your successor needs to be more gifted than you.*

church is gone!" she demanded. The chairman quickly responded, "Ma'am, the man who established and built this church died and rose again two thousand years ago. He's still here with us and I think we'll do just fine."

They have done more than just fine. In fact they have done awesome. And if I had it to do over again I wouldn't change anything about that.

THREE KEYS TO TRANSITIONING OUT SUCCESSFULLY

In retrospect I see three important keys to a successful transition for the person stepping aside: First, *set a date well in advance and stick to it*. Ministers fool themselves into thinking, "I'll sense when it's time to retire." It sounds noble to say, "I'm going to keep going as long as God is using me and then I'll quit." But stepping down is such a difficult and emotional decision that almost everyone delays it years beyond what is best.

Secondly, *be willing to swallow your pride repeatedly.* For a transition to be successful your successor needs to be more gifted than you. Otherwise he won't be able to lead the church to the next level. If you help choose and train a gifted successor your ego will invariably be wounded at times. People will praise him and not you. Your successor may become too aggressive and offend you or he does things differently and it works!

I remember the day my secretary asked me if I could do a funeral on Friday and I said, "No, I'm sorry but I have an appointment Friday morning that I can't break. Would you see if Dave Stone can do it?" She sheepishly admitted, "Well, Dave was their first choice and he couldn't do it either. He wondered if you could." Being second choice can hurt your pride.

When our church hired Kyle Idleman as our third teaching pastor, he was only twenty-six. The congregation was intrigued with Kyle because he preached with no notes. It was impressive. He didn't ramble or forget. He was an excellent communicator with good content and constant eye contact.

Friends would tease me in the hallway, "Hey! How long you been preaching and you still use notes? That kid uses no notes when he preaches. That's incredible, don't you think?" I'd flash a fake smile and agree.

One day Denny Crum, former coach of the University of Louisville basketball team, said to me, "Hey, Bob, I'm going up to Indianapolis next Saturday to the John Wooden Classic. I know you've always wanted to meet Coach Wooden—why don't you ride up with me?" I jumped at the chance. Kyle was preaching that weekend and I thought, "At least I won't have to listen to people bragging about Kyle preaching with no notes."

I stopped in Kyle's office the next day to tell him I wouldn't be in the Saturday evening service because I was going to be in Indianapolis where I'd have an opportunity to meet John Wooden. Kyle said, "That's great. Tell Coach Wooden I said hi." Somewhat puzzled, I asked, "Do you know Coach Wooden?" He said, "Oh, yeah. When I was an associate minister at the Shepherd of the Hills Church in California Coach Wooden was a member there."

I want to Indianapolis, met Coach Wooden and had a nice conversation with him. Toward the end of our discussion I said, "Coach, a guy named Kyle Idleman said to tell you hello." Coach Wooden responded, "Kyle Idleman! You know he's the only preacher we ever had that didn't use notes when he preached."

The retiring leader has to ask, "Do I want this organization to succeed or do I want my ego stroked?" The Bible says, "Do nothing out of selfish ambition or vain conceit. Rather, in humility value others above yourselves, not looking to your own interests but each of you to the interests of the others" (Philippians 2:3–4).

The third key to a meaningful transition is to *retire* to *something and not* from *something*. An exhausted minister who was on the verge of retirement was asked what he was going to do with his extra time. He quipped, "The first year I'm just going to sit on the front porch in a rocking chair." "Then what?" he was asked. "Then the second year I'm going to start rocking," was his response.

If that's your concept of retirement you're going to be miserable. There's a direct correlation between your sense of purpose and your self-worth. If you have nothing significant to do your lack of purpose will drag you into a pit of despair.

When I retired ten years ago I didn't want to sit in a rocking chair all day. I still planned to be active in ministry. I have plenty to do every day. I conduct monthly mentoring retreats for pastors, preach about forty weekends a year, prepare Bible study videos for small groups, write a weekly blog, and am now writing my second book for Moody. I can't imagine waking up with nothing to do. The last ten years have been the most enjoyable and most rewarding decade of my life.

Retirement should be regarded as a period of service, not indulgence. The Bible is full of examples of people who made their most significant contribution after age sixty-five. Moses was eighty when he led the Israelites out of slav-

> *"I must be a crazy old man. I'm ninety-four and I just bought a new trombone."*

ery. Caleb was eighty-five when he led the Israeli army into battle. Sarah was ninety when she gave birth to Isaac. Anna was eighty-four when she identified the baby Jesus as the Messiah. The apostle John was over eighty when he wrote Revelation.

History is full of examples also. Colonel Sanders was nearly broke when he used his first Social Security check at age sixty-five to start Kentucky Fried Chicken. Ronald Reagan was seventy-three when elected president for the second time. Billy Graham preached to national television audiences at age ninety.

Sam Rosenberg was still playing the trombone in our church orchestra at ninety-four. He once told me, "I must be a crazy old man. I'm ninety years old and just bought a new trombone." His doctor said that's probably why he lived so long and was so healthy. He exercised his lungs and had a sense of purpose.

John Piper cites a number of historical figures, such as Ben Franklin, who began new assignments at advanced ages. Piper concluded, "So all you boomers just breaking into Medicare, gird up your loins, pick up your cane, head for the gym and get fit for the last lap. Fix your eyes on Jesus' face at the finish line. There will be plenty of time for R and R in the resurrection. For now there's happy work to be done."[2]

Well said. But Jesus said it even better when He challenged us: "Be faithful, even to the point of death, and I will give you the crown of life."

TWO FINAL CHALLENGES TO PREACHERS

A good character is the best tombstone. Those who loved you, and were helped by you, will remember you. So carve your name on hearts, and not on marble.

—C. H. SPURGEON

In my opinion there are two words that summarize what it takes to be an effective minister over the long haul. The first is *faithful*. Just be faithful to God's calling regardless of people's response to your efforts.

Satan's primary weapon against ministers is not lust or greed but discouragement. The ministry can be disheartening at times. Criticism, indifference, disappointment, loneliness, betrayal, stress and exhaustion can overwhelm you. Like Elijah hiding in the cave or Moses nursing his wounds in the wilderness, you're tempted to whine, "I've had enough! I quit!"

But don't lose heart. Hear again the Lord's challenge, "Be faithful, even to the point of death, and I will give you life as the victor's crown" (Revelation 2:10). Remember this world is not your home. You have a hope that can never perish, spoil or fade kept in heaven for you. People are not your ultimate judge. God's Word promises: "Let us not become weary in doing good, for at the proper time we will reap a harvest if we don't give up" (Galatians 6:9).

One of the tests of faithfulness is can you take a punch? Are you tough enough to get back up when you're knocked down? The Bible encourages us, "Consider him who endured such opposition from sinners, so that you will not grow weary and lose heart. In your struggle against sin, you have not yet resisted to the point of shedding your blood" (Hebrews 12:3–4).

Woody Allen was certainly no theologian, but he was right when he suggested that 80 percent of success is just showing up. Sometimes the way we tell the Lord we love Him is to get out of bed, put our feet on the floor, and go about our daily assignments, even though we don't feel like it. That's called faithfulness.

The second word that summarizes effective ministry is *joy*. Be joyful. It's one thing to get back up when knocked down; it's another to continue to serve with a joyful countenance and a positive spirit.

An oft-overlooked characteristic of effective ministers is that they enjoy life. They are happy, vibrant people. I don't always agree with Joel Osteen's approach to ministry, but if there's one thing the rest of us ought to learn from the popularity of Joel Osteen it's the value of preaching with a winsome smile and a cheerful spirit. The Scripture commands us to be joyful in all circumstances and rejoice in the Lord always. Isaiah promised, "I will bestow on them a crown of beauty instead of ashes, the oil of joy instead of mourning, and a garment of praise instead of a spirit of despair" (Isaiah 61:3).

Dietrich Bonhoeffer grew up in privileged circumstances. He spent the last eighteen months of his life in prison, deprived of all but the basic necessities of life. He was not yet forty years old. He had every reason to be dour.

But listen to this description of Bonhoeffer from Payne Best, another prisoner: "He always seemed to me to diffuse an atmosphere of happiness, of joy in every smallest event in life, and of deep gratitude for the mere fact he was alive . . . He was one of the very few men that I have ever met of whom his God was real and ever close to him . . . he was quite calm and normal, seemingly perfectly at ease . . . his soul really shone in the dark desperation of our prison." Best added that Bonhoeffer "had always been afraid that he would not be strong enough to stand such a test but now he knew there was nothing in life of which one need ever be afraid. He was also cheerful, ready to respond to a joke."[1]

If Dietrich Bonhoeffer could be joyful in a brutal, rat-infested Nazi prison, you and I can be joyful in our most difficult circumstances—if we really believe what we say we believe.

Years ago doctors Frank Minirth and Paul Meier wrote a book with the memorable title *Happiness Is a Choice*. I believe that premise. You choose to be happy or you choose to be miserable. It's a daily choice. You can't always control the emotions that churn on the inside but can control your countenance, your words, your actions—what is seen externally.

William James is said to be the father of modern psychology. He said a lot of things I don't agree with. But he said one thing I really like. "If you act the way you wish you felt you'll eventually feel the way you act." That's similar to Rick Warren's suggestion to "Fake it 'til you make it." It's much easier to act yourself into a way of feeling than to feel yourself into a way of acting.

If you don't feel joyful, act joyful. If you don't feel happy, get happy. Once in a great while you can step onto the platform and moan, "Folks, pray for me today. I've had a rough week and I'm really down. I need your support." And the congregation will rally to your cause. But that doesn't work very often. Jesus said, "When you fast don't let the world know you're fasting, wash your face, comb your hair, put on a cheerful countenance to the world." That's not hypocrisy, that's obedience.

Be upbeat with your body language. Let your countenance radiate with the grace of Christ. Smile warmly as you quote, "This is the day the Lord has made, let us rejoice and be glad in it!" and go on. Just hours before He died Jesus told His disciples, "I have told you this so that my joy may be in you and that your joy may be complete" (John 15:11). No wonder His disciples would go through a wall for Him.

No one wants to be around a whiner. No one ever says, "After church let's go over to Bill's house—I just love to hear him gripe." No, we're attracted to people who are joyful. When you faithfully speak the truth with a spirit of joy it's contagious. It lifts the spirits of others and is more likely to make you feel better in the end.

One Sunday morning, early in my ministry, I referred to the German composer Wagner and mistakenly pronounced his name phonetically, like a dog's tail. A refined musician met me at the door and snipped, "It's 'Vahg-ner'. . . please!" She was right, of course. But I felt put down and went home discouraged, nursing feelings of inadequacy. "Maybe this country boy doesn't belong in this sophisticated, city environment. I'm in way over my head."

But I chose to be faithful and get back up when knocked down. I decided I wouldn't let one uppity snob rob me of my joy. The following Sunday I found a way to squeeze into my sermon a lighthearted apology to the congregation, "I'm sorry that last Sunday I mentioned the German composer 'Wagner' in my sermon. I've since learned that I didn't pronounce his name correctly. It is pronounced 'Vagner'—I know 'cause I looked it up in Vebster's dictionary!"

I smiled. The congregation burst out laughing with me. And we went on for forty more years. You can go on too. Don't quit. Don't get discouraged by slight offenses or seemingly insurmountable problems. Be faithful in preaching God's Word and loving God's people. Be faithful to your God-given wife and children. And do it with a joyful spirit. Laugh at yourself and be of good cheer since Jesus has overcome the world!

And if you act the way you wish you felt, you will eventually feel the way you act. Because "Those who go out weeping, carrying seed to sow, will return with songs of joy, carrying sheaves with them" (Psalm 126:6).

BOB RUSSELL
Louisville, Kentucky

APPRECIATION

The fact that I remained in the same church for forty years and have been in ministry over fifty years is evidence of God's grace and forgiveness. I'm thankful the Lord has blessed me far beyond what I ever dreamed or imagined. I'm also grateful for the daily encouragement and understanding I received from my wife, Judy, and my sons Rusty and Phil, and their families. I'm deeply indebted to dozens of church elders and staff members who were supportive and often protected me and encouraged me. These people were like Aaron and Hur, Moses's associates, who held up his arms in battle when he grew weary. Thanks to all of you in leadership at Southeast Christian Church who shared in so many spiritual victories. "To God be the glory, great things He hath done."

NOTES

Chapter 1—I would minister more by faith ...

1. J. Oswald Sanders, *Spiritual Leadership* (Chicago: Moody, 2007), 48.

2. Corrie ten Boom, *Clippings from My Notebook* (Nashville: Thomas Nelson Inc., 1982).

Chapter 2—I would watch less television ...

1. Matthew Sleeth, MD, *24-6* (Carol Stream, IL: Tyndale House, 2012).

Chapter 3—I'd pay less attention to criticism ...

1. J. Oswald Sanders, quoted in A. R. Stager, "Thick Skin, Soft Heart," gardensdontlaunch.wordpress.com, August 6, 2013, https://gardensdontlaunch.wordpress.com/2013/08/06/thick-skin-soft-heart/.

2. Danny Meyer, "Service Is King." *Sky*, December 2014, *deltaskymag.com*.

Chapter 4—I'd be kinder ...

1. Bruce Larson, *Dare to Live Now!* (Grand Rapids: Zondervan, 1978).

2. Quoted in Gordon MacDonald, *Rebuilding Your Broken World* (Nashville: Thomas Nelson Inc., 2004), 40.

Chapter 7—I would never again attempt to cover over ...

1. Ty Grigg, "How I Learned to Stop Worrying about the Billy Graham Rule and Love Like Jesus," July 18, 2014 (www. missioalliance.org/how-I-learned-to-stop-worrying-about-the-billy-graham-rule-and-love-like-jesus).

Chapter 8—I would maintain preparation ...

1. Nicholas Carr, "The Web Shatters Focus, Rewires Brains," May 24, 2010, wired.com www.wired.com/2010/05ff_nicholas_carr/May.

2. Joanne Cantor, PhD, *Conquer Cyber-Overload* (Cyber Outlook Press, 2009).

3. Fred Craddock, *Overhearing the Gospel: Revised and Expanded Edition* (Atlanta: Chalice Press, 2002), 94.

Chapter 9—I would make the necessary adjustments . . .

1. Oswald Chambers, *My Utmost for His Highest*, quoted in Kenneth Boa, *Conformed to His Image* (Grand Rapids: Zondervan, 2001), 272.

Chapter 10—I would again laugh a lot . . .

1. D. Elton Trueblood, *The Humor of Christ* (New York: Harper & Row, 1975).

2. Webb Garrison, *The Preacher and His Audience* (Westwood, NJ: Fleming H. Revell Company, 1954), 192.

3. James Thompson, *Preaching Like Paul* (Atlanta: Westminster John Knox Press, 2000).

Chapter 12—I would avoid getting caught up . . .

1. Quoted in Politico.com, August 8, 2008.

2. Donald Campbell, *Decoder of Dreams* (Wheaton, IL: Victor Books, 1979), 22.

Chapter 14—I would stay in one place . . .

1. Joel Gregory, *Too Great a Temptation* (Chicago: Summit Publishing Group Legacy Books, 1994).

2. John Piper, "What Happens When You Turn 65," *World* magazine, May 7, 2011.

Two Final Challenges to Preachers

1. Eric Metaxas, *Bonhoeffer* (Nashville: Thomas Nelson Inc., 2011), 514.

ACKNOWLEDGMENTS

1. To Duane Sherman, Moody's Acquisitions Editor for Strategic Partnerships, for initiating the concept for this book and encouraging me to proceed.
2. To my super-supportive wife, Judy, for listening to ideas for each chapter and sharing her judicious perspective.
3. To my minister friends, Phil LeMaster, Mark Jones, Roy Roberson, Dave Kennedy, and my son Rusty, who took time to read the raw material and offer helpful suggestions.
4. To Dr. Matthew Sleeth, who took time to read the unedited version of this work and offered keen insights and meaningful encouragement.
5. To Betsey Newenhuyse—my editor, who has been a joy to work with and whose superb editing skills are much needed and appreciated.
6. To Jack Graham, exceptional pastor of one of America's finest churches, for taking time to write such a gracious foreword and being such an encouragement to me.
7. To a host of elders at Southeast Christian who, like the first elders in Numbers 11, helped me "carry the burden of all the people."

8. To Dave Stone and a multitude of associate ministers at Southeast Christian Church, who, like Aaron and Hur in Exodus 17, have held up my hands in the spiritual battle.

9. To Don Waddell, my executive assistant, and his secretary, Emily Engelhardt, who free up my time for writing by tending to ministry details and have been a Godsend to me in this "retirement" chapter of my life.

10. To Debbie Carper, whose unsurpassed proofreading skills have been a continual blessing to me for nearly thirty years.

"I thank my God every time I remember you."
Philippians 1:3

ABOUT THE AUTHOR

God has blessed Bob Russell with a life much different than one he could have ever imagined. As a young man growing up in northern Pennsylvania, Bob had intended on becoming a high school basketball coach in his hometown. During his senior year of high school, however, Bob realized a desire in his heart to enter the ministry. Soon thereafter, he enrolled in Cincinnati Bible Seminary, where he graduated in 1965.

At just twenty-two years of age, Bob became the pastor of Southeast Christian Church. That small congregation of 120 members became one of the largest churches in America, with 18,000 people attending the four worship services every weekend in 2006 when Bob retired. Now through Bob Russell Ministries, Bob continues to preach at churches and conferences throughout the United States, provide guidance for church leadership, mentor other ministers and author Bible study videos for use in small groups. An accomplished author, Bob has written over a dozen books, including *Acts of God* (Moody, 2015).

Bob and his wife of fifty years, Judy, have two married sons, Rusty and Phil. Rusty Russell is the Lead Pastor of the New Day Christian Church in Port Charlotte, Florida, after serving at Southeast for many years. Phil Russell is a Sergeant with the

Louisville Metro Police Department as well as a film actor with the Screen Actors Guild. Bob and Judy have seven grandchildren with whom they enjoy spending their time.

Bob also enjoys playing golf and is an avid University of Louisville football and basketball fan.

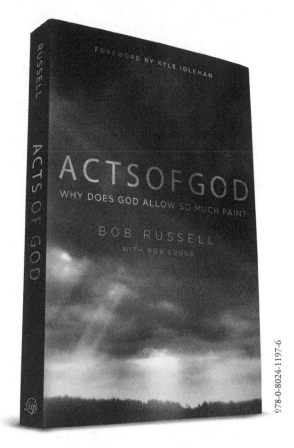

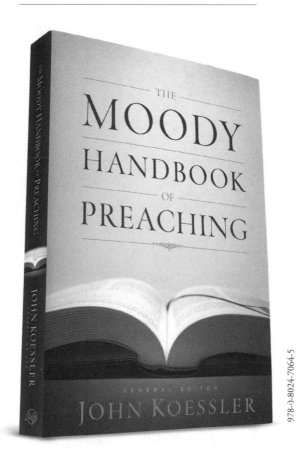